I0449766

Critical Issues in Justice and Politics

Volume 6 Number 1   May 2013
ISSN 1940-3186

Copyright © 2013 Critical Issues in Justice and Politics
ISBN 978-1-300-96964-8

Editorial Contents – The contents of each article are the views, opinions, or academic inferences of the individual article author. Publication of each article may not reflect the views or positions of the journal, the department, or Southern Utah University. All material is published within the spirit of academic freedom and the concepts of free press.

Editorial Office

Department of Political Science and Criminal Justice
Southern Utah University
351 University Blvd., GC406
Cedar City, UT 84720

Phone: 435-586-5429
Fax: 435-586-1925
University Webpage: http://www.suu.edu/
Department Webpage: http://www.suu.edu/hss/polscj/
Journal Webpage: http://www.suu.edu/hss/polscj/CIJP.htm

Managing Editor
Ryan Yonk

Associate Editor
Sandi Levy

Editorial Board Members
David Admire - Department Chair – Phone: 435 586-1926; Office GC406J

Political Science
Randy Allen – Phone: 435 586-7949; Office: GC 406E
John Howell – Phone: 435 865-8093; Office: GC 406H
G. Michael Stathis – Phone: 435 586-7869; Office: GC 406K
Ryan Yonk – Phone: 435 586-7961; Office: GC 406M

Criminal Justice
Terrie Bechdel – Phone: 435 865-8613; Office GC 406G
Carl Franklin – Phone: 435-586-5410; Office: GC 406L
Terry Lamoreaux – Phone: 435-865-8043; Office: TH 109
John Walser – Phone: 435-586-7980; Office: GC 406F
Ron Flud – Phone: 435-586-1921; Office: GC 406A

Office Manager
Sandi Levy – Phone: 435-586-5429; Office: GC 406E

Critical Issues in Justice and Politics

Volume 6 Number 1   May 2013   ISSN 1940-3186

Contents

Articles

Subscription Information

Critical Issues in Justice and Politics is a refereed (peer-reviewed) journal which contributes to the theoretical and applied nature of justice and politics. We are a scholarly journal which requires all articles to undergo an extensive review process for both content and format. Our emphasis is on the exchange of qualified material in order to generate discussion and extend the often limited boundaries of scholarly exchange.

Critical Issues in Justice and Politics is sponsored by the Department of Political Science and Criminal Justice at Southern Utah University. The editorial board is comprised of faculty from the department as well as select faculty and practitioners from around the United States.

Published twice a year (March and September) *Critical Issues in Justice and Politics* focuses on emerging and continuing issues related to the nature of justice, politics, and policy. A special emphasis is given to topics such as policy, procedures and practices, implementation of theory, and those topics of interest to the scholar and practitioner alike.

Nature of Electronic Publication:

Critical Issues in Justice and Politics is considered a serials publication under definitions by the Library of Congress and the International Standard Serial Number (ISSN) system. The ISSN number, along with identifying information for the serial publication, appears on all copies of the journal. The journal may be obtained online or through many of the traditional research databases in academia.

Because we publish online we provide a wider audience than most small, scholarly journals. The cost of other journals can be restrictive; often making purchase and use of the journal difficult for the average faculty member. With our electronic format we provide access to the journal at no cost to qualified subscribers. This provides a larger audience with increased opportunity for those who wish to publish.

Copies are distributed via email and online access to subscribers first. Authors receive access to the electronic copy and may purchase print copies.

We are an electronic journal which is published using the Portable Document Format (PDF).

Submission Guidelines

Critical Issues in Justice and Politics welcomes submissions from anyone who can write a high quality scholarly article. We are especially interested in scholarly, critical, and constructive articles which focus on an emerging or continuing issue is justice and politics. We also seek review essays (reviews of recent literature on a given topic), reports of significant justice or political issues, book reviews, and position papers worthy of scholarly review and comment.

It is the editorial policy of *Critical Issues in Justice and Politics* to accept submissions from all disciplines so long as the material relates to justice and politics. We also encourage submissions from practitioners, students, and others who have an interest in the topics.

Simultaneous Submissions

We prefer manuscripts which are not under review by other journals or publications. We endeavor to review all manuscripts in a timely fashion, so simultaneous submissions are not usually necessary. Refereed submissions are submitted within forty-eight hours of acceptance and we generally ask reviewers to complete their assignment within 10 working days. In most instances an editorial decision may be reached within a month of submission.

Non-refereed materials usually receive attention within the first week of submission. An initial editorial decision is often made within 5 business days.

All papers submitted for refereed publication will be sent to at least two reviewers. We use a blind-review process which submits papers in anonymous format. If there is a clear split between the reviewers then a third reviewer may be used when necessary for clarification or additional comment. We do rely very heavily on our reviewers for insight and recommendations. All of our reviewers hold the appropriate degree and experience to qualify them for the particular project.

Reviewers are asked to evaluate manuscripts on the basis of their scholarly competence as well as the potential contribution to appropriate theory or related areas. Authors may not contact reviewers during the process, and reviewer names are not disclosed unless the reviewer agrees for such disclosure.

Authors who dispute the findings or suggestions of a reviewer may submit their response in writing. Final decisions on publication remain the domain of the editorial board.

For more information or to submit an article or other material for review please see our webpage.

Journal Webpage: http://www.suu.edu/hss/polscj/CIJP.htm

From the Editor

This issue of Critical Issues in Justice and Politics presents an innovative set of articles in line with our new, broader editorial mission. That mission seeks to provide a multi-disciplinary outlet for research and scholarship focused on questions of Justice and Politics and how those concepts operate in the real world. From Koehle's analysis of private security options for storage facilities to larger questions of justice and security in Roquen's evaluation of international stability and security, the authors featured in this edition have addressed these questions from a variety of methodological and theoretical approaches.

As always we wish to thank the reviewers, authors, and especially our associate editor, Sandi Levy, for her tireless work in turning out this edition of the journal. As we push forward with our editorial mission big things are coming for CIJP starting with the fall 2013 edition. While our editorial process will remain identical and the standards to which we hold our authors and reviewers remain high, we expect to begin publishing the e-version as an open access journal. Unlike many e-journals we will not charge authors a publishing or submission fee. We will continue to publish the journal twice a year generally in April/May and Nov/Dec. Print editions will remain subscription based and a small fee will be necessary to cover printing and binding costs. We expect this change to broaden the reach of our Journal allow the articles we publish a wider distribution and impact.

Best,

Dr. Ryan M. Yonk
Managing Editor, Critical Issues in Justice and Politics

DARK GEOPOLITICS: THE BEIJING-MOSCOW NEXUS IN SUDAN AND SYRIA

Jeff Roquen
Lehigh University

Since the fall of the Soviet Union, China and Russia have made dramatic progress in restoring their former alliance (prior to the Sino-Soviet split in 1960) over parallel geopolitical interests. While most scholars of international relations have viewed their reconstituted relationship as a largely abstract device to balance the unipolar (or hegemonic) power of the United States, the burgeoning policy coordination between Beijing and Moscow has been concretely employed to strategically lock up key resources (oil and minerals) for the purposes of expanding their economies, strengthening their regimes, and promoting malleable dictatorships abroad. In order to understand the recent humanitarian crises in Sudan and Syria, the African roots and global ramifications of the new Sino-Russian alliance must first be explored and analyzed. By tracing the recent histories and exposing the converging interests behind each regime over the past three decades, this paper illuminates the origins and interrelationship of the genocide in Darfur and the civil war in Syria.

On 26 September 2012, British Prime Minister David Cameron took the podium at the General Assembly of the United Nations and made an extraordinary set of remarks. To the delegates in the room and the world at large via television, radio and the Internet, Cameron charged,

> "The blood of these young children is a terrible stain on the reputation of this UN. And in particular, a stain on those who have failed to stand up to these atrocities and in some cases aided and abetted Assad's reign of terror."[1]

Although the Prime Minister did not directly single-out the two nations he had castigated for supporting Syrian President Bashar Al-Assad's murderous war against his own people, the world fully understood the import of his condemnation. Cameron was reproving Beijing and Moscow for their joint-efforts in blocking UN resolutions to place an arms embargo on Syria and impose sanctions.

---

[1] Jason Grove, "'Blood on their hands:'Cameron blames Russia and China for torture and killing Syrian children under Assad's 'terror reign'"*The Daily Mail* (UK) 26 September 2012 Accessed 29 October 2012 http://www.dailymail.co.uk/news/article-2209057/David-Cameron-UN-Russia-China-blood-Syrian-children-hands.html

Jeff Roquen is a PhD student in the Department of History at Lehigh University.

More than fifty years since their political fallout, China and Russia have slowly but surely re-aligned since the fall of the Soviet Union in 1991. Most scholars of international relations have viewed their rapprochement as an abstract device to balance the unipolar (or hegemonic) power of the United States. Yet, the re-establishment of close policy coordination between Beijing and Moscow has resulted not only as a means to counter US influence but as a geopolitical strategy to lock up key minerals and sources of oil for the purposes of expanding their economies, strengthening their regimes, and promoting allied, malleable dictatorships abroad. Over the past fifteen years, the unprecedented thrust of China into Africa exemplifies this approach. In order to fully understand the origins and the trajectory of the recent humanitarian crises in Sudan and Syria, it is necessary to retrace the making of the new Sino-Russian alliance and examine the geopolitical agenda behind their partnership. By exposing the elements of realpolitik behind the coordinated policies of Beijing and Moscow in Khartoum and Damascus, policymakers, analysts and modern historians will be able to gain insight for the purpose of reassessing the locus, diffusion and dynamics of power and interest across three distinct yet politically linked regions.

The Falling Out of Beijing and Moscow After The Second World War

In 1945, Chinese Communist leader Mao Zedong, who had waged an insurgency against the nationalist regime of Chiang Kai-shek prior to expediently banding together to drive the Japanese army from China, bristled at Soviet Premier Josef Stalin's continued support for his rival after the defeat of the Empire of Japan. Despite their shared commitment to Marxist ideology, Stalin held Mao at bay in a bid to shape post-war East Asia. Upon emerging triumphant in China's civil war, Mao could have made a decisive break with his Russian patron in 1949. Due to fearing an assault on his new government by American forces, however, he made a two-month pilgrimage to Moscow to shore up relations. His efforts paid off. Only a few months later, a newly-minted agreement - the Sino-Soviet Treaty of 1950 - provided Beijing with much sought-after economic aid and security guarantees.[2]

The diplomatic honeymoon did not last long. By the time Nikita Khrushchev denounced Stalin for his dictatorial policies and ruthless purges of the Communist Party at a closed door session of the party elite in 1956, Mao had made considerable progress in constructing a highly authoritarian system for the People's Republic of China. Hence, Beijing and Moscow were beginning to move in opposite directions.

---

[2] John Lewis Gaddis, *We Now Know: Rethinking Cold War History* (Oxford: Clarendon Press, 1997), 64-65.

Under the Great Leap Forward in 1958, China embarked on a new five-year economic plan that subordinated small farmers to large-scale producers for the purpose of supporting rapid industrialization. Rather than a surge in the economy, the Chinese peasantry, which had been cut off from its means of subsistence, was utterly decimated from Mao's man-made, widespread famine. As Moscow neither supported Mao's departure from Soviet economic orthodoxy nor his decision to shell the Kuomintang-controlled island of Jinmen (or Quemoy in English), relations between the two countries began to deteriorate. At a conference in Romania in June 1960, Soviet representatives openly denounced the CCP for its economic and military heresy. Shortly thereafter, Moscow dramatically recalled all of its technical advisors from its Communist ally and backed out of "many existing agreements."[3] By the end of the decade, the Sino-Soviet Treaty of 1950 was in tatters, and palpable tension existed along the 2,500 mile border between the two countries. War, along with the possibility of a nuclear exchange, was not out of the question.[4]

One year after the People's Republic of China (Beijing) supplanted the Nationalist regime of Chiang Kai-Shek (Taiwan) in the UN Security Council (1971), US President Richard Nixon and Secretary of State Henry Kissinger seized the opportunity to cultivate relations with Mao. Although Nixon did not win any assistance from Chinese leaders in ending the Vietnam War, his week-long presence in the Celestial Kingdom succeeded in widening the rift between Beijing and Moscow. Due to its well-documented repression of its citizens, six years passed before Jimmy Carter, who became the first American head of state to substantively base American foreign policy on human rights, granted China official US recognition in 1978. Over the next three and a half decades, his decision proved to be both ironic and tragic.[5]

China, Russia & Sudan: The Intersection of Power and History

The political relationship between Beijing and Moscow, which has been marked by periods of generous cooperation and bitter dissention since the conclusion of the Second World War, has come full circle over shared geostrategic interests in Africa. Similar to the imperial era prior to the First World War, Africa, which endured the so-called "Scramble" between Britain,

---

[3] Michael Dillon, *China: A Modern History* (London: I.B. Taurus, 2010), 322.

[4] Tony Saich, *Governance and Politics of China* (New York: Palgrave, 2001), 24-36; Dillon, *China: A Modern History*, 343.

[5] James Mann, *About Face: A History of America's Curious Relationship with China from Nixon to Clinton* (New York: Alfred A Knopf, 1998), 38-50, 79-92; Robert F. Drinan, *Cry of The Oppressed: The History and Hope of Human Rights Revolution* (San Francisco: Harper & Row, 1987), 80-93.

Germany, France, Portugal and other European powers for territorial conquest and control from 1884-1914, has attracted a resurgence of foreign interlopers in the form of oil and mining companies in a zero-sum quest for economic resources in recent decades. Indeed, the meteoric rise of China's economy has not only turned Africa into a battleground for Western (US and Europe) and Eastern (China and Russia) influence, but it has also recast the dynamics of the international order for the twenty-first century.

Since the restructuring of the Chinese economy toward a market-oriented model beginning in the late 1970s, China's economy has grown exponentially. In 1980, China's economy began to surge and posted a remarkable GDP of 7.8%. For a country as populous as China and one with an unparalleled internal market, relative stagnation had been the order of the day during the last years of Mao's rule. From 1960-1978 (Mao died in 1976), the annual GDP has been calculated to have been an underperforming 5.3%.[6]

How dramatic has the Chinese economic turnaround been? According to a World Bank study, the market reforms begun by former Chinese leader Deng Xiaoping (1904-1997) and continued by his successors have reduced poverty levels by 55% in only thirty years. Hence, an astounding 500 million Chinese have been able to climb out of indigence and into the lower rung of the middle-class (or higher) since 1980. At its current pace, China will overtake the US as the largest economy in the world by 2030 – if not by 2020.[7] In order to power its rapidly expanding cities and booming economy, China began looking for oil outside of the politically turbulent Middle East in the 1990s. As Africa had been estimated to have more than 100 billion barrels of oil reserves within five key nations, a new "scramble" between East (China) and West (US & European) oil companies ensued. For China, the historically fractured and war-torn country of Sudan suddenly became its geopolitical focus.[8]

---

[6] "China GDP: how it has changed since 1980," The Guardian (UK) Datablog (no date) Accessed 31 October 2012 http://www.guardian.co.uk/news/datablog/2012/mar/23/china-gdp-since-1980

[7] The World Bank: Developmental Research Center of The State Council, the People's Republic of China "China 2030: Building a Modern, Harmonious, and Creative High-Income Society," Washington, DC, 2012 Accessed 20 November 2012 http://www.worldbank.org/content/dam/ Worldbank/document/China-2030-complete.pdf; In April 2011, the IMF predicted China would overtake the US as the world's largest economy in 2016. As the Chinese and the world economy has again stagnated after a brief post-2008 recession expansion, that date now seems improbable – although Chinese economic ascendancy may still occur well before 2030. See David Gardner, "The Age of America ends in 2016: IMF predicts the year China's economy will surpass US' The Daily Mail (UK) 25 April 2011 Accessed 31 October 2012 http://www.dailymail.co.uk/news/ article-1380486/The-Age-America-ends-2016-IMF-predicts-year-Chinas-economy-surpass-US.html

Since attaining independence more than a half a century ago, Sudan has been wracked by internal conflict and plagued by unstable governments.[9] In 1983, the country drifted into its second civil war as the largely non-Muslim Sudanese People's Liberation Movement (SPLM) took up arms against Khartoum for its attempt to sever the south into three provinces to dilute its political power.[10] Even worse was yet to come. Six years later, a relatively unknown army officer, Umar Hasan Ahmed al-Bashir, formed a secret coterie of likeminded officers and successfully toppled the regime. Prime Minister Sadiq al-Mahdi, who had led the coalition government, was imprisoned along with dozens of other politicians and unsympathetic army officers. Shortly after the coup d'état, Bashir set up a Revolutionary Command Council (RCC) to run the nation according to the religious strictures of Islamist Hasan al-Turabi and the National Islamic Front – the radical Islamist coalition behind Bashir. By 1991, revisions in Sudan's Sharia law effectively subjugated women and decreed that any and all forms of dissent would be treated as apostasy – a crime punishable by death.[11]

Thirty years earlier, the American oil giant Chevron made an initial geological foray into Sudan and discovered areas containing rich oil deposits. Due to Bashir's brutal repression of recalcitrant ethnic groups in the south and his sponsorship of terrorism (Al-Qaeda mastermind Osama Bin-Laden received sanctuary from Bashir for a time), the Clinton administration imposed sweeping economic sanctions on Khartoum. Trade between the United States and Sudan was prohibited.[12] For Beijing and its rapidly expanding economy in need of oil, this was an opportunity. Twelve months after Western companies pulled out, China National Petroleum Corporation (CNPC) bought into the Greater Nile Petroleum Operating Company consortium (40%) and undertook oil production in three oil blocks in the south, where most of the deposits were located.[13] In

---

[8] Michael T. Klare, *Rising Powers, Shrinking Planet: The Global Assault on Africa's Vital Resources* (New York: Metropolitan Books, 2008), 150. Klare is a top-notch scholar and an expert on geopolitics and the global economy. This work, along with his others, demonstrates impeccable research and trenchant analysis.

[9] Klare, *Rising Powers, Shrinking Planet*, 152 Sudan achieved independence in 1956.

[10] Mohamed H. Fadlallha, *Short History of Sudan* (Lincoln, Nebraska: iUniverse, 2004), 49-50.

[11] Robert O. Collins, *A History of Modern Sudan* (Cambridge: Cambridge University Press, 2008), 185-191. As most media outlets refer to al-Bashir as simply Bashir, the Sudanese president will be referred to as Bashir forthwith.

[12] Klare, *Rising Powers, Shrinking Planet*, 166; Pak K. Lee, Gerald Chan and Lai-Ha Chan, "China in Darfur: Humanitarian Rule-Maker or Rule Taker?" *Review of International Studies* Vol. 38, Issue 2 (April 2012), 431.

[13] Ibid., 430-431.

short order, CNPC, along with its Malaysian and Indian partners in the consortium, constructed pipelines to carry the oil from its blocks in southern Sudan to the Red Sea for shipment. In approximately eighteen months, China had successfully courted the Bashir government, acquired oil production rights, built a viable oil-export infrastructure across Sudan and began counting on the country for more than five percent of its oil imports.[14]

From its spike in oil revenue in the late 1990s and early 2000s, Khartoum readily purchased military hardware – largely from China and Russia - to both fortify its regime and to carry out brutal campaigns against non-Muslim populations. Tragically, the stage had been set for the first acts of genocide in the twenty-first century.[15]

Drawing Lines East and West: The Rise of the New Beijing-Moscow Axis

When the Soviet Union officially ceased to exist at the end of 1991, the international relations world of bipolarity suddenly became unipolar. As the United States stood as the only nation capable of projecting power to any significant degree around the world, democracy and capitalism were presumed by more than a few observers to have been epochally triumphant. In the year that witnessed the fall of the Berlin Wall and a massive uprising in Tiananmen Square in Beijing (1989), one bright new scholar of world affairs, Francis Fukuyama, declared "The End of History" in a much debated essay by the same name.[16] New words and old words began to enter and re-enter the English lexicon to describe the new order dominated by Washington. America was suddenly characterized as a "superpower" (the remaining one), a "hyperpower" (used more among European intellectuals) or a "hegemon" (a default term widely used by international relations scholars). If democracy and capitalism were the twin pillars of a global future beyond history, neither Beijing nor Moscow received the full message. Less than a year after the fall of Lenin and Stalin's grand social engineering experiment, Qian Qichen, the Foreign Minister of China, stated, "The USA's *hegemonic* stance and its attempts to interfere in the internal affairs of other states pose the greatest danger to socialist China." (italics added)[17] His statement was not only a defense of China's militant crackdown on

---

[14] David H. Shinn, "China's Deft Sudan Diplomacy" *The Diplomat* 19 September 2012 Accessed 1 November 2012 http://thediplomat.com/china-power/chinas-deft-sudan-diplomacy/

[15] "China's Arms Sales To Sudan" Fact Sheet" *Human Rights First* (no pagination) Accessed 1 November 2012 http://www.humanrightsfirst.org/wp-content/uploads/pdf/080311-cah-arms-sales-fact-sheet.pdf

[16] Francis Fukuyama, *The End of History and The Last Man* (New York: Free Press, 1992) Fukuyama's seminal article appeared in *The National Interest* in 1989 and was expanded and turned into a book three years later.

widespread protests in Tiananmen Square (Beijing) and elsewhere around the country on 4 June 1989 – in which hundreds or perhaps thousands of peaceful demonstrators died at the hands of a ruthless assault by the Chinese military but also a projection of China's future foreign policy.[18] In order to counter American influence, Qian further stated the need to band with several regional nations – including Russia.[19]

In 1996, Beijing launched the Shanghai Cooperation Organization (SCO) with Moscow as a co-sponsor. This bloc of states, which originally included Kazakhstan, Tajikistan and Kyrgyzstan, later enrolled Uzbekistan. In more recent years, it has also awarded "observer status" to India, Iran, Mongolia and Pakistan. While the SCO has entertained talks concerning human trafficking, terrorism, border control and boundary disputes, its ultimate purpose has been to provide an official arena for discussions and deals on energy and security.[20] Although initially ignored or dismissed as a largely hollow organization by Washington, the SCO has become closely monitored by the Department of State and European diplomats due to its functional expansion. Beyond serving as a broker for major contracts involving oil and weaponry, the SCO has developed into a formidable geopolitical alliance. As China, Russia and their new regional partners have effectively managed to challenge the IMF, alter US plans on missile defense for Eastern Europe and conduct joint-military exercises over the past decade, the restoration of ties between Beijing and Moscow has been nowhere more pivotal than in Africa – particularly Sudan.[21]

The Poisoned Fruit of The Beijing-Khartoum Alliance: Darfur

The origins of the genocide in Darfur between the Islamist Sudanese government and the Fur – an ethnic, religiously syncretic group in western Sudan – have long roots. While the north and east have been far more influenced by Islam for centuries, the west and south have remained largely pluralistic in

---

[17]Quoted in Michael L. Levin, *The Next Great Clash: China and Russia vs The United States* (Westport, CT: Praeger, 2008), 98.

[18] Mara Hvistendahl, "The Great Forgetting: 20 Years After Tiananmen Square" *The Chronicle of Higher Education* 19 May 2009 Accessed 1 November 2012 http://chronicle .com/article/The-Great-Forgetting-20-Ye/44267

[19] Levin, *The Next Great Clash*, 98.

[20] Ivan Campbell et. al "China and Conflict: Affected States: Between Principle and Pragmatism" *Saferworld* January 2012 Accessed 2 November 2012 http://www.saferworld. org.uk/downloads/pubdocs/China%20and%20conflict-affected%20states.pdf Levin, *The Next Great Clash*, 108.

[21] Michael Moran, "Putin: The Company He Keeps" *Slate* 5 June 2012 Accessed 2 November 2012
http://www.slate.com/blogs/the_reckoning/2012/06/05/putin_the_company_he_keeps.html

language and belief. After Bashir and the National Islamic Front came to power in 1989, Khartoum began an earnest campaign against the independent, multiethnic Fur peoples five years later by administratively redistricting the region to diminish their political representation.[22] This, however, was a first and temporary expedient. In partnering with China to develop its oil sector, the Sudanese government was able to tap into a lucrative source of revenue essential to the ultimate designs of its regime. By 2004, China had become the lead investor in Sudan's oil industry. Simultaneously, Beijing and Khartoum concluded several significant business agreements to allow Chinese companies to administer and finance key infrastructure projects in Sudan – including two hydroelectric plants and a dam.[23]

Ties between the two countries quickly proliferated. From 2003-06, the amount of oil delivered from Sudan to China spiked sixty-three percent. One year later, Beijing monopolized a full forty percent of Sudanese output. Khartoum's coffers were overflowing.[24] Bashir quickly cemented his bilateral relationship with Beijing by promising to award additional business to Chinese construction companies and to purchase a sizable number of Chinese-manufactured weapons. As oil shipments skyrocketed, China gladly supplied Sudan with $55 million in small arms. Beyond light weaponry, Sudan also acquired hundreds of military trucks, several tanks, and as many as twenty "Fantan fighter-bombers" from China in these years (2003-06). Along with military hardware, China also lent Sudan a number of advisors and fighter-pilot trainers.[25]

What was the reason behind Khartoum's heavy investment in Chinese weaponry? In the radical-Arab Janjaweed militia, Khartoum had found mercenaries willing to assist the Sudanese Armed Forces in launching a campaign of extremist violence. During the peak years of their economic and trade relationship, Sudan used its newfound wealth and its newly-acquired cache of weapons from China to conduct a policy of extermination against Darfur. By 2007, 300,000-400,000 Darfurians had been slaughtered and two million others displaced by the Bashir-sponsored rape and murder of the Fur people. The scale

---

[22] Robert O. Collins, *A History of Modern Sudan*, 280-284.

[23] Michael L. Levin, *The Next Great Clash*, 114-115.

[24] Moira Herbst, "Oil for China, Guns for Darfur" *Businessweek* 14 March 2008 Accessed 5 November 2012 http://www.businessweek.com/stories/2008-03-14/oil-for-china-guns-for-darfurbusinessweek-business-news-stock-market-and-financial-advice

[25] "China's Arms Sales To Sudan: Fact Sheet" *Human Rights First* (no pagination) Accessed 5 November 2012 http://www.humanrightsfirst.org/wp-content/uploads/pdf/080311-cah-arms-sales-fact-sheet.pdf ; Hilary Andersson, "China 'is fueling war in Darfur'" *BBC NEWS* 13 July 2008 Accessed 5 November 2008 http://news.bbc.co.uk/2/hi/7503428.stm

and scope of these atrocities remain incomprehensible. On a visit to the region in 2005, Don Cheadle and John Prendergast recounted the scene,

> During our visit to Darfur and the Darfurian refugee camps in Chad, we heard story after story of mind-numbing violence perpetrated by the Sudanese government army and the Janjaweed militias they support. We heard of women being gang-raped, children being thrown into fires, villages and communities that had existed for centuries being burned to the ground in an effort to wipe out the livelihoods and even the history of those communities.[26]

Day after day, reports of the genocide leaked out of Sudan in 2003. After the Sudanese Liberation Army (SLA) and the Justice and Equality Movement (JEM) united to defend Darfur and regional nomads under attack, the issue became known to the wider world.[27] One year later, a first step was taken to quell the violence.

On 30 July 2004, the UN Security Council passed a resolution directly condemning Khartoum. More importantly, it demanded the Sudanese government immediately cease its campaign of violence and placed a weapons embargo on the regime. Despite overwhelming evidence to the contrary, Beijing completely denied its role in supplying weapons to Bashir.[28] Although the Sudanese government did allow the UN to enter the country to provide humanitarian assistance shortly after the UN resolution, Khartoum remained undaunted, and the SAF and Janjaweed continued their brutal assaults on Darfur with a range of

---

[26] Don Cheadle and John Prendergast, *Not On Our Watch: The Mission To End Genocide In Darfur And Beyond* (New York: HarperCollins, 2007), 7-8; In 2008, one news report chronicled the misfortunes of Kaltam Abakar Mohammed in Darfur. She personally witnessed three of her seven children "being blown to pieces" by a Chinese fighter jet. See Hilary Andersson, "China 'is fueling war in Darfur'" *BBC NEWS* 13 July 2008 Accessed 5 November 2012 http://news.bbc.co.uk/2/hi/7503428.stm

[27] "Genocide in Darfur" *United Human Rights Council* (no pagination) Accessed 6 November 2012 http://www.unitedhumanrights.org/genocide/genocide-in-sudan.htm Salih Booker and Ann Louise-Colgan, "Genocide in Darfur" *The Nation* 12 July 2004 Accessed 6 November 2012 http://www.thenation.com/article/genocide-darfur

[28] UN Security Council, Security Council Resolution 1556 (2004) on measures to prevent the sale or supply of arms and related materiel, 30 July 2004, S/RES/1556 (2004), available at: http://www.unhcr.org/refworld/docid/411355bc4.html [accessed 6 November 2012]; "China's Arms Sales To Sudan" Fact Sheet" *Human Rights First* (no pagination) Accessed 6 November 2012 http://www.humanrightsfirst.org/wp-content/uploads/pdf/080311-cah-arms-sales-fact-sheet.pdf

imported Chinese arms. On 18 September, The UN Security Council again took action. In a new resolution (1564), the Council 1) invited the African Union (AU) into Sudan to act as monitors on the frontlines, 2) called for a political solution to the conflict between Khartoum and "The Sudan People's Liberation Movement," 3) requested the presence of UN human rights monitors in order to investigate potential acts of genocide and 4) demanded identification and punishment for those responsible for atrocities.

Beyond these provisions for ending the conflict, operative clause number fourteen was undoubtedly of the greatest concern to both China's ambassador to the United Nations and leaders in both Khartoum and Beijing. In that provision, the Security Council members threatened to "*consider* taking additional measures…such as actions to affect Sudan's petroleum sector and the Government of Sudan or individual members of the Government of Sudan."[29] This was indeed a backhanded swipe at one of the UN Security Council members – China – for its unscrupulous trade of oil and guns with Khartoum prior to and during the genocide campaign in Darfur. In response, Beijing registered its official abstention on the resolution. As a permanent member of the Security Council, China subsequently used its prospective veto power over the next three years to dilute the content of fourteen UN Security Council resolutions to shield itself and its premier oil client from punitive legal action and economic sanctions for directly promoting, aiding and abetting war crimes.[30]

Under the glaring spotlight of sponsoring genocide, Beijing and Khartoum intensified their collaboration to ward off international criticism. In the spring of 2005, President Hu of China and President Bashir of Sudan held a private meeting at the Asia-Africa Summit in Jakarta and issued a statement pledging to "push forward the friendly cooperative relations between the two countries."[31] Two years later, China not only continued to hold UN sanctions against Sudan at bay by insisting on Khartoum's "sovereignty" over its own internal affairs but it also simultaneously funded the construction of an elaborate presidential palace for Bashir.[32] From its official policy of "non-interference"

---

[29] UN Security Council, Security Council Resolution 1564 (2004) on Darfur, Sudan, 18 September 2004, S/RES/1564 (2004), available at: http://www.unhcr.org/refworld/docid/41516da44.html [accessed 6 November 2012]

[30] Richard Cockett, *Sudan: Darfur and The Failure of an African State* (New Haven: Yale University Press, 2010), 224; Ivan Wheeler et al., "China and Conflict – Affected States: Between Principle and Pragmatism" *Saferworld* January 2012 Accessed 6 November 2012 http://www.saferworld.org.uk/downloads/pubdocs/China%20and%20conflict-affected%20states.pdf

[31] Michael T. Klare, *Rising Powers, Shrinking Planet*, 167.

[32] "Chinese leader boosts Sudan ties" *BBC NEWS* 2 February 2007 Accessed 6

Table 3: EU 2004 Turnout Regression with Controls (continued)

	Coefficient	SE	T
Catholic	-2.89	21.67	-.13
Previous Members	-5.08	19.64	-.26
Proximity of Country Elections	120.4	99.53	1.21

** $p < .05$ * $p < .1$
N=25 R^2=.7874**

The addition of controls and previous members to the regression results in an increase in the explanatory value of the model but it results in fewer significant variables. The addition of these variables does support that when there is a larger percentage of Catholic population in a specific country, there will be a related lower voting turnout of that country's population. Additionally, members prior to the 2004 expansion have a decreased turnout in the EU elections. This is consistent with the findings in Table 1. Further, these findings support earlier discussion that turnout is declining in the EU. However, it is surprising that the countries who have been exposed to the EU longer do not have higher turnout, as they would be more educated (due to longevity in the Union) about the organization. Nonetheless, turnout in the new countries could be higher because of recent admittance and potentially more recent exposure to the workings of the EU electoral system. What was expected was that because the new member countries were admitted just prior to the 2004 election that there would be little difference in the turnouts of these groups.

An interesting and important finding of Table 3 is that proximity of national elections has a positive impact on turnout; thus, the more years between the previous national election and the EU election, the higher the turnout for individual countries. This is important because it demonstrates that the findings tells election planners that election fatigue is an important consideration in the EU electoral turnout.

Conclusion

This research has shown that there is a connection between education/ knowledge and electoral turnout. When looking at the process of electoral engineering or changing systems, an important consideration is educating the public on the new system. This process of education must include education on the electoral system but also of the governmental body itself. Further, understanding the system is just one component of this research. Trust is another important component of this education. Institutions need to instill confidence in the population. This trust and confidence is necessary to provide programs to the state but also in order to get the population to support them. While trust is insignificant and in the opposite direction than expected, the relationship between trust in the EU and voter turnout needs further investigation to completely understand what is going on and if there is something that is not being addressed through that variable.

When discussing the turnout for the EU it is important to note that the closeness of national elections to the EU elections can affect turnout. Luxembourg is the exception to the case; however, other EU countries demonstrate voter fatigue when there are multiple elections in close proximity to one another. Furthermore, new member states are not the only EU countries with low turnout, previous members of the EU have experienced decline in turnout. The EU needs to address this issue in order to maintain the legitimacy of this organization.

The EU needs to consider several things if they hope to achieve higher turnout for their elections. First, they need to build trust in the institution. Second, they must listen to the public desires on expansion of the EU and on the EU Constitution – the failure of the EU to be responsive to the public has created distrust and disdain for the organization, which has resulted in lower turnout. Third, the EU needs to be mindful of national elections and have EU elections when they are least affected by national elections to limit voter fatigue. Finally, and most importantly, the EU needs to educate its citizens on the EU itself. Increased citizen education on the EU can only lead to increased turnout and trust in the EU.

Future Research

This study is limited because it is looking at individual countries as the unit of analysis and at a superimposed governmental system. Future research in the area of political knowledge and electoral turnout in new systems could be explored at the individual level. Being able to measure individual turnout and individual knowledge levels could only strengthen the importance of this research. Another fruitful area of research could focus on the individual state governments and the impact of their domestic situation on the political knowledge of the European Union.

References

Aspinwall, Mark. 2002. "Preferring Europe: Ideology and National Preferences on European Integration" *European Union Politics,* Vol. 3, No. 1, 81-111.

Birzea, Cesar. "European Citizenship as a Cultural and Political Construct" http://www.jsse.org/2005-se/birzea_european_citizenship.htm

Blondel, Jean, Richard Sinnott and Palle Svensson. 1998. *People and Parliament in the European Union: Participation, Democracy and Legitimacy.* Oxford: Clarendon Press.

and respect for "sovereignty," China has attempted to both justify and veil its collaboration with tyrannical regimes around the globe in the pursuit of key natural resources and profit.[33] Under the calculus of "noninterference," China's officially sanctioned arms manufacturers have reaped significant profits over the last decade. In 2010, Beijing became the fourth largest exporter of arms in the world, and all but two percent of its shipments were delivered to developing nations. After South Asia (57%), and the Middle East (21%), Africa was third in the reception of Chinese-made guns.[34]

That same year marked a move by the United Nations to formally accuse Beijing of clandestinely supplying Khartoum with ammunition for its war against the people of Darfur. As the evidence would have implicated China of violating UN imposed sanctions, Beijing expressed outrage at the highest diplomatic levels and considered using its weighty vote to prevent the publication of a UN report containing evidence of its complicity in fueling the African genocide.[35] Between its foreign policy of non-interference and its employment of denial and deception, Beijing has been able to partially camouflage the nature of its relationship with the Sudanese regime.[36]

Sudan's Other Enabler of Genocide

China, however, has not been the only violator of the UN sanctions against arms exports to Sudan. At the same time, the governments of Russia and Belarus have also supplied Bashir with weaponry. While Beijing has primarily focused on funneling significant amounts of small arms (although it has sold Fantan fighters and other aircraft to Sudan), Moscow and Minsk have furnished heavier military hardware. Since the beginning of the conflict in Darfur, the

---

November 2012 http://news.bbc.co.uk/2/hi/6323017.stm

[33] Ivan Wheeler et al., "China and Conflict – Affected States: Between Principle and Pragmatism" *Saferworld* (January 2012), 10. Accessed 6 November 2012 http://www.saferworld. org.uk/downloads/pubdocs/China%20and%20conflict-affected%20states. pdf In stating "China supports the development of democracy and the rule of law in Africa. But we never impose our will on others," Premier Wen Jiabao was using carefully constructed rhetoric to rationalize and justify Beijing's partnership with tyrannical states. (See above, page 10)

[34] Ibid., (no pagination)

[35] Colum Lynch, "China fights UN report on Darfur" *The Washington Post* 10 October 2010 Accessed 8 November 2012 http://www.washingtonpost.com/wp-dyn/content/article/2010/10/15/AR2010101506100.html

[36] In 2006, Smith College professor Eric Reeves rightly stated, "China's behavior in oil exploration…(has) been marked by deep complicity in gross human rights violations, scorched-earth clearances of the indigenous populations in the oil regions, and direct assistance to Khartoum's regular military forces." See Michael T. Klare, *Rising Powers, Shrinking Planet*, 167.

governments of Russia and Belarus have delivered at least thirty-six Mi-36 and Mi-17 helicopters, more than a dozen Sukhoi 25 jets, several types of armored vehicles and a number of air-to-ground rockets. Instead of following in the footsteps of Beijing by dispatching flight instructors to Sudan, Russia has moved in the opposite direction and gone one step further. It has brought pilots of the Sudanese Armed Forces to its Air Force base in Torzhok (Russia) for training on military aircraft sold to Khartoum.[37]   Ultimately, the decision of China and Russia (and Belarus) to provide substantive military support to Sudan has resulted in continued war atrocities and a destabilization of the entire region.

In early 2011, the SAF (Sudanese Armed Forces) intensified its attacks on Darfur due to fear of losing control of the region to the SPLA (Sudan People's Liberation Army) and the emergent state of South Sudan. Military attack helicopters (Mi-24) and jet fighters (Su-25) from Russia were not only used to suppress resistance groups but to conduct "indiscriminate aerial bombardments and the clearing and burning of villages in eastern Darfur."[38]   Consequently, refugee camps swelled with the addition of 70,000 civilians forced to abandon their homes. As talks between Khartoum and JEM (Justice and Equality Movement) continued to break down over the ensuing months, NGOs on the ground struggled to cope with the dire situation.[39] The world's attention and much of the mainstream press has abandoned the plight of the peoples of Sudan, yet the same crimes, which had prompted an outpouring of media coverage and activism worldwide in 2005, were still being committed by the same perpetrators (Sudan and its client-militias) in 2011, and Moscow (along with Beijing) was able to

---

[37] Colum Lynch. "China fights UN report on Darfur" *The Washington Post* 16 October 2010 Accessed 8 November 2012 http://www.washingtonpost.com/wp-dyn/content/article/ 2010/10/15/ AR2010101506100.html ; Amnesty International "Sudan: No End To Violence in Darfur – Arms Supplies Continue Despite Ongoing Human Rights Violations" (9 February 2012): 18. Accessed 8 November 2012 http://www.amnestyusa.org/sites/default/files/afr540 072012en.pdf ; Amnesty International "Darfur: New Weapons from China Fuelling Conflict" 8 February 2012 Accessed 8 November 2012 http://www.amnesty.org/ en/news/darfur-new-weapons-china-and-russia-fuelling-conflict-2012-02-08; Human Rights First, "China's Arms Sales To Sudan," 1-2. Accessed 8 November 2012   http://www.human rightsfirst.org/wp-content/uploads/pdf/080311-cah-arms-sales-fact-sheet.pdf

[38] Amnesty International "Sudan: No End To Violence In Darfur" (9 February 2012), 9; Amnesty International Darfur: New Weapons from China Fuelling Conflict" 8 February 2012 Accessed 8 November 2012 http://www.amnesty.org/en/news/darfur-new-weapons-china-and-russia-fuelling-conflict-2012-02-08

[39] Larisa Epatko, "In Darfur, Violence Grows in Darfur as Flashpoint Town Abyei Arms," *PBS Newshour*, 1 April 2011 Accessed 8 November 2012 http://www.pbs.org/newshour/ rundown/ 2011/04/darfur-and-abyei.html

continue supplying Khartoum with weapons despite a UN embargo by simply denying its involvement.[40]

China, Russia and The Maturation of The Shanghai Cooperation Organization

In May 2012, the annual G8 Summit was held at Camp David, Maryland. Rather than attend as the newly-elected, returning head of state, Russian President Vladimir Putin sent his protégé and predecessor Dmitry Medvedev to represent Moscow. It was not only a deliberate move but also a signal of Russia's continued gravitation toward an adversarial bloc of predominantly eastern, non-aligned, non-democratic states.[41] One month later, Putin arrived in Beijing to play an equally prominent role with the host country in a meeting of the Shanghai Cooperation Organization (SCO). On his eighth visit to the Chinese capital in twelve years, Putin was an animated figure at the three-day conference. When the foreign minister of Iran labeled the United States and its allies "arrogant powers" on the first day, Russia's president took the podium to express his wholehearted agreement.[42]

Over the last decade, the burgeoning relationship between Beijing and Moscow has been re-forged by shared commitments to supplying arms to non-democratic (and mostly tyrannical) regimes around the world and through expanding bilateral trade – including arms transfers between the two countries. In the second year of the genocide in Darfur (2004), China increased its purchases of Russian arms by thirty-two percent from the previous year. In 2005, both Beijing and Tehran took clandestine (or almost clandestine) deliveries on twenty Russian missiles. Iran also purchased Russian "Tor M1 surface-to-air missiles" along with "upgrades" for its Russian-made fighter planes. The rapid expansion of military ties between China and Russia in the 2000s also resulted in the sale of diesel submarines and missile systems from the latter to the former (2002) and the first "Sino-Russian joint military exercise" (2005).[43]

---

[40] Amnesty International "Sudan: No End To Violence In Darfur" (9 February 2012), 9; Amnesty International Darfur: New Weapons from China Fuelling Conflict" 8 February 2012 Accessed 8 November 2012 http://www.amnesty.org/en/news/darfur-new-weapons-china-and-russia-fuelling-conflict-2012-02-08

[41] "Putin flexes muscle in shunning US-hosted G-8 talks" *Reuters* 10 May 2012 Accessed 9 November 2012 http://www.reuters.com/article/2012/05/10/russia-putin-usa-idUSL5E8GA7N820120510

[42] Chen Qin, "Why Putin is betting on China," *Marketwatch* 10 June 2012 Accessed 9 November 2012 http://articles.marketwatch.com/2012-06-10/economy/32154774_1_sino-russian-relations-russian-president-vladimir-putin-sino-russian-ties; Michael Moran, "Putin: The Company He Keeps" *Slate* 5 June 2012 Accessed 9 November 2012 http://www.slate.com/blogs/the_reckoning/2012/06/05/putin_the_company_he_keeps.html

In purely economic terms, Russia's largest and most significant relationship is with China. Trade between Beijing and Moscow, which centers on exchanges of military hardware, armaments and energy, and consumer items, exceeded $80 billion in 2011. That figure is projected to surpass $100 billion in 2015 and $200 billion in 2020. Interestingly, an increasing number of their economic transactions are being done in their respective currencies rather than in standard US dollars. Hence, mutual economic interest, anti-Western nationalism and regional security have all factored into the Beijing-Moscow alliance.[44] In a meeting between President Putin and President Hu Jintao of China at the June 2012 Shanghai Cooperation Organization (SCO) conference, Hu stated, "better and more intimate relations between China and Russia are a blessing for the two countries and to the world."[45] For the people of western Sudan and Syria, however, the Beijing-Moscow military-foreign policy alliance has been nothing short of a curse over the past decade.

Going South and East: China, Russia, South Sudan and Syria

Due to its prodigious economic growth, rapid urban expansion and unprecedented increase in manufacturing, China requires an ever-increasing amount of oil to power its productive engine. In less than a decade, China will overtake the European Union and the United States to become the largest importer of oil in the world. Over the next two decades, China's oil imports will rise from slightly more than five million barrels of oil per day (bbl) to nearly thirteen million bbl. In order to meet future demands, Beijing will undoubtedly tap its three largest suppliers in Africa (Angola, Sudan and the Republic of the Congo) to an even larger degree. Indeed, it is doing so already.[46] In its quest for oil in Africa, China has made significant oil-for-infrastructure-investments in several oil-rich countries, and it has expanded its trade with Africa by more than

---

[43] Michael Levin, *The Next Great Clash*, 98-112.

[44] Fred Weir, "Putin's China visit shows warming ties between neighboring giants," *The Christian Science Monitor* 4 June 2012 Accessed 9 November 2012 http://www.csmonitor.com/World/Europe/2012/0604/Putin-s-China-visit-shows-warming-ties-between-neighboring-giants; "Russia and China cement business alliance" *RT* 6 June 2012 Accessed 9 November 2012 http://rt.com/business/news/china-russia-cement-deals-investment-046/

[45] Chen Qin, "Why Putin is betting on China," *Marketwatch* 10 June 2012 Accessed 9 November 2012 http://articles.marketwatch.com/2012-06-10/economy/32154774_1_sino-russian-relations-russian-president-vladimir-putin-sino-russian-ties

[46] Christopher Alessi, "Expanding China-Africa Oil Ties," *Council on Foreign Relations* 8 February 2012 Accessed 12 November 2012 http://www.cfr.org/china/expanding-china-africa-oil-ties/p9557 ; *The World Factbook 2012*. Washington, DC: Central Intelligence Agency, 2012 Accessed 12 November 2012 https://www.cia.gov/library/publications /the-world-factbook/rankorder/2175rank.html

300% since becoming the continent's number one trade partner (surpassing the United States) four years ago.[47]

For years, China has bankrolled Khartoum in its genocidal war against Darfur for the purpose of maintaining its drilling rights and major investments in oil infrastructure in the southern half of the country. When the South began to break away politically from Khartoum with the backing of the international community in 2011-12 after decades of civil unrest, China quickly changed course. As its alliance with Khartoum threatened to jeopardize its oil interests in the new state of South Sudan, Beijing made a strategic *volte face* and began courting the new regime in Juba to ensure the sanctity of its oil contracts.[48] Upon gaining independence on 9 July 2011, South Sudan agreed to a 50-50 oil-sharing revenue deal with Khartoum. Yet, the exact percentage and logistics of carrying oil to northern ports remained unresolved.[49] Six months after becoming a new nation, a crisis unfolded over one of the thorny issues in the oil agreement. In a row over transit fees, Juba demonstrated its leverage by closing down all but two percent of its production of oil. Due to China's immediate diplomatic response, a return to hostilities and the possibility of an all-out war was averted.[50] In April 2012, South Sudan President Salva Kiir arrived in Beijing for talks surrounding their shared economic and political interests in the region. Only three and a half weeks later, Beijing and Juba announced an $8 billion oil-for-infrastructure agreement "to build roads, bridges and telecom networks, and to develop agriculture and hydroelectric power" for the fledgling nation.[51] Similar to its $2

---

[47] Ty McCormick, "What does China want for its $20 billion to Africa?," *Foreign Policy* 19 July 2012 Accessed 19 July 2012 http://blog.foreignpolicy.com/posts/2012/07/19/is_china_acting_responsibly_in_africa China's trade with Africa reached $166 billion in 2011.

[48] Pak K. Lee, Gerald Chan and Lai-Ha Chan, "China in Darfur: Humanitarian Rule-Maker or Rule-Taker?" *Review of International Studies* Vol. 38/Issue 02/April 2012, 432-433. Accessed 12 November 2012 http://journals.cambridge.org/action/displayAbstract;jsessionid=BB1A26933DDC889CAC69F0DAFB204301.journals?fromPage=online&aid=8527349

[49] "South Sudan Faces Hurdles As World's Newest Country," *IMF Survey Magazine: Countries and Regions* The International Monetary Fund 18 July 2011 Accessed 12 November 2012 http://www.imf.org/external/pubs /ft/survey/so/2011/car071811a.htm

[50] In the weeks and months prior to and after South Sudan became independent, Sudan waged a low-intensity war against its southern neighbor by supporting armed proxy groups that carry out "indiscriminate bombings." See Ross Mountain, "The Republic of South Sudan turns a new page – but humanitarian needs persist," *The Guardian* (UK), 8 July 2011 Accessed 12 November 2012 http://www.guardian.co.uk/world/2011/jul/08/sudan-darfur-aid-south-kordofan-independence

[51] "South Sudan 'agrees $8bn deal with China' *BBC NEWS* 28 April 2012 Accessed 12 November 2012 http://www.bbc.co.uk/news/world-africa-17883321; "China's New Courtship in South Sudan," *International Crisis Group* 4 April 2012 Accessed 12 November 2012

billion oil-for-infrastructure deal with Angola almost a decade earlier, China clearly intends to continue using the same trade model for the foreseeable future.[52] Beyond making significant diplomatic overtures to South Sudan, China also dramatically ended its unwavering support of Khartoum in the United Nations. Rather than prevent passage of UN Security Council Resolution 2046 in May 2012, which called for both sides to cease and desist from all cross-border attacks, Beijing voted to approve the measure.[53]   In the words of former Australian Prime Minister Kevin Rudd, "China identifies Africa as an alternative source of energy and raw materials that are essential to the continuation of China's economic modernization process."[54] As such, Beijing has and will pursue an expedient foreign policy that caters to primarily to resource-acquisition.

At the same time China was attempting to mend the rift between Khartoum and Juba in 2011, an "Arab Spring" rocked the Middle East with revolutions from below in a number of countries. As Egyptians conducted massive demonstrations in Tahrir Square in Cairo against the corrupt, authori-tarian regime of Hosni Mubarak, the heavily repressed population of Syria revolted against the iron-clad rule of Bashar al-Assad.[55] While the West expressed its collective diplomatic outrage at the heavy-handed tactics being used to quell the uprisings, China remained tactically aloof and Russia rushed to protect Assad. Syria has remained in the Russian geopolitical orbit since the days of being ruled by Hafez al-Assad (Bashar's father). Beyond receiving nearly $20 billion in Russian investments for development of its domestic

---

http://www.crisisgroup.org/en/regions/africa/horn-of-africa/south-sudan/186-chinas-new-court
ship-in-south-sudan.aspx

[52] See Indira Campos and Alex Vines, "Prospects for Improving U.S.-China-Africa Cooperation," *Center for Strategic and International Studies* March 2008, 6-9 Accessed 12 November 2012 http://csis.org/files/media/csis/pubs/080306_angolachina.pdf

[53] James Traub, "The Accidental Peacemaker," *Foreign Policy* 4 May 2012 Accessed 12 November 2012 http://www.foreignpolicy.com/articles/2012/05/04/the_accidental_peacemaker; UN Security Council, Security Council resolution 2046 (2012) [on the situation in Sudan and South Sudan] , 24 May 2012, S/RES/2046(2012) , available at: http://www.unhcr.org/refworld/docid/4fbe0206195.html [accessed 12 November 2012]

[54] Kevin Rudd, "Viewpoint: China and the world," *BBC NEWS* 8 November 2012 Accessed 12 November 2012 http://www.bbc.co.uk/news/world-asia-china-20217333

[55] David D. Kirkpatrick and Kareem Fahim, "Mubarak's Allies and Foes Clash in Egypt," *The New York Times* 2 February 2011 Accessed 13 November 2012 http://www.nytimes.com/ 2011/02/03/world/middleeast/03egypt.html?pagewanted=all&_r=0; Elizabeth Flock, "Syria Revolution: A revolt brews against Bashar al-Assad's regime," *The Washington Post* 15 March 2011 Accessed 13 November 2012 http://www.washingtonpost.com/ blogs/blogpost/post/syria-revolution-revolt-against-bashar-al--assads-regime/2011/03/15/ABrw   NEX_blog.html   The Egyptian and Syrian revolts began in earnest in February 2011 and March 2011 respectively.

energy, tourism and infrastructure in 2009 alone, Syria also agreed in principle to purchase $5 billion worth of weapons from Russian arms-makers in early 2012. Aside from maintaining a lucrative client for guns and military hardware, Moscow is especially interested in checking Western influence in the region by holding onto Tartus – its last naval base on the Mediterranean. In fact, Russia has employed 600 engineers to rebuild the aging naval station during the ongoing Syrian civil war.[56]

Rather than attempt to take a balanced approach or camouflage its real-politik, Moscow has boldly supported the Assad regime despite its grievous violations of human rights. In October 2011, Russia used its Security Council member status in the United Nations to thwart an attempt by the diplomatic body to condemn Assad's murderous campaigns against civilians – including women and children.[57] Three months later, Moscow not only prevented the UN Security Council from taking action but it also dispatched an "aircraft-carrying missile-cruiser" with "a consignment of Yakhont cruise missiles" to bolster Assad's hold on power.[58] Under protection of Moscow's veto power in the UN Security Council, Assad has been able to carry on his limitless campaign of violence and repression with arms from Russia and Iran.[59] On 3 February 2012, Assad's forces waged an all-out assault on the town of Homs after a long siege. At least two hundred residents were slaughtered in a scene of carnage reminiscent to the destruction of the town of Hama by Hafez al-Assad three decades earlier.[60] Undaunted by its failure to override previous Russian objections, the UN again attempted to take action in the hours immediately after this latest atrocity. Although Moscow took the lead, Beijing prominently joined its Shanghai Cooperation Organization (SCO) partner to block the making of a new resolution

---

[56] Daniel Treisman, "Why Russia protects Syria's Assad," *CNN* 3 February 2012 Accessed 13 November 2012 http://www.cnn.com/2012/02/02/opinion/treisman-russia-syria/index.html

[57] Human Rights Watch, *World Report 2012: Syria* Accessed 13 November 2012 http://www. hrw.org/world-report-2012/world-report-2012-syria Assad and his henchmen murdered approx-imately 3,500 civilians – including children – in one brutal assault in 2011.

[58] Daniel Treisman, "Why Russia protects Syria's Assad," CNN 3 February 2012 Accessed 13 November 2012 http://www.cnn.com/2012/02/02/opinion/treisman-russia-syria/index.html

[59] "Russia threatens Syria resolution at UN" *BBC NEWS* 18 January 2012 Accessed 13 November 2012 http://www.bbc.co.uk/news/world-middle-east-16609789

[60] Ben Quinn, "Syria: more than 200 dead after 'massacre' of Homs," 3 February 2012 *The Guardian* (UK) Accessed 13 November 2012 http://www.guardian.co.uk/world/2012/feb/04/syria-report-homs-killings; Barack Obama, "Statement by the President on Syria," 4 February 2012 *The White House* Accessed 13 November 2012 http://www.whitehouse.gov/the-press-office/2012/02/04/statement-president-syria

to call Assad to accountability. Similar to their involvement in Sudan, Beijing and Moscow have joined hands over Syria to protect their respective anti-democratic, geopolitical ambitions.[61]

Conclusion

In July 2008, the International Criminal Court (ICC) in The Hague issued a warrant for the arrest of Omar al-Bashir. In the indictment, the president of Sudan was charged with "five counts of crimes against humanity," "two counts of war crimes," and "three counts of genocide" for his campaign against Darfur.[62] Rather than assisting the international community in bringing him to justice, China's leadership welcomed Bashir to Beijing for high-level talks in June 2011 to sign a set of new finance and trade agreements.[63] On 11 November 2012, former ICC prosecutor Luis-Moreno Ocampo stated that NATO had the grounds and authority to issue an arrest warrant for Syrian President Bashar al-Assad for his role in the killing of innocent, unarmed civilians.[64] Barring a large-scale NATO military intervention, however, Assad will be able to keep his regime of terror in power indefinitely with shipments of Russian weapons and continued diplomatic protection against UN sanctions by Beijing and Moscow.[65]

---

[61] Holly Yan, "Why China, Russia won't condemn Syrian regime," *CNN* 5 February 2012 Accessed 13 November 2012 http://articles.cnn.com/2012-02-05/middleeast/world_meast_syria-china-russia-relations_1_syrian-president-bashar-al-assad-syrian-government-syrian-regime?_s=PM:MIDDLEEAST; Ted Piccone and Emily Alinikoff, "Rising Democracies Take on Russia and China," *The National Interest* 17 February 2012 http://nationalinterest.org/commentary/rising-democracies-take-russia-china-6525 In exchange for China's support of Syria's control of the Golan Heights, Syria has backed China's 'One China' policy with respect to Taiwan.

[62] International Criminal Court, "ICC 02/05-01/09 The Prosecutor v Omar Hassan Ahmad Al Bashir," Accessed 15 November 2012 http://www.icccpi.int/en_menus/icc/situations%20and%20cases/situations/situation%20icc%200205/related%20cases/icc02050109/Pages/icc02050109.aspx ; International Criminal Court, "Situation in Darfur, Sudan - In The Case Of The Prosecutor v. Omar Hassan Ahmad Al Bashir" 4 March 2009 (First Arrest Warrant) Accessed 15 November 2012 http://www.icc-cpi.int/iccdocs/doc/doc639078.pdf

[63] "UN Criticizes China's Failure to Arrest Sudan's Bashir," *Voice of America* 29 June 2011 Accessed 15 November 2012 http://www.voanews.com/content/un-criticizes-chinas-failure-to-arrest-sudans-bashir---124771729/141530.html

[64] "NATO could arrest Assad in Syria:ex-ICC prosecutor," *The Nation* 11 November 2012 Accessed 15 November 2012 http://www.nation.com.pk/pakistan-news-newspaper-daily-english-online/national/11-Nov-2012/nato-could-arrest-assad-in-syria-ex-icc-prosecutor

[65] Bessma Momani, "Russia and China Provide Cover for Assad's Syria," *The Toronto Star* 31 January 2012 Accessed 15 November 2012 http://www.thestar.com/opinion/editorialopinion/article/1124472--russia-and-china-provide-cover-for-assad-s-syria

In the course of the last decade, Beijing and Moscow have formed a lethal alliance to counter Western influence. By aligning their interests with the criminal regimes of Omar al-Bashir in Sudan and Bashar al-Assad in Syria, China and Russia have emphatically opted to carry out a foreign policy of realpolitik rather than one based on international law.[66] Indeed, their expedient, Machiavellian approach to world politics lies in stark contrast to one of principled, long-term stability. As such, British Prime Minister David Cameron was entirely correct to condemn their actions in his speech to the United Nations. As long as the international community fails to sanction the Beijing-Moscow power nexus, the predatory politics of guns and oil will continue to undermine all efforts to bring democracy and human rights to both Africa and the Middle East – and ultimately sunder the credibility of the United Nations and its pledge to create a world order based on justice.

---

[66] Thomas Wheeler, "China's Development Diplomacy," *The Diplomat* 4 March 2012 Accessed 15 November 2012 http://thediplomat.com/2012/03/04/china%E2%80%99-develo pmentdiplo macy/ In writing "when the benefits are seen to favor certain groups or consolidating the power of elites China's economic role may inadvertently exacerbate instability," Wheeler clearly understated the base motives and baleful consequences of Beijing's economic and political investments in dictatorships.

EDUCATION AND TURNOUT IN NEW ELECTORAL SYSTEMS: THE EUROPEAN UNION CASE

Shauna Reilly
Northern Kentucky Universisty

This paper investigates the connection between civic literacy and voter turnout in European Union elections, by focusing on how voter political knowledge contributes to their overall participation in European elections. This paper also investigates other factors that contribute to participation in EU elections such as state ideology, voter fatigue and length of membership. The main finding of this paper is that political knowledge (as measured in this paper) has little impact on the turnout in EU elections. However, issues of support (for constitution, political union and enlargement) do have some impact on the turnout in these elections.

Scholars of electoral engineering argue that there are institutional structures that influence electoral outcomes and suggest that there are better ways of structuring electoral systems (namely forms of proportional representation). What are the consequences of changing electoral systems on the electorate and their participation rates? To change electoral systems there would be significant institutional change but the electorate must absorb this change as well. Citizens need to be educated (again) on their electoral systems. This is a long involved process, expensive to implement and not always effective.

This essay will explore the political knowledge of European Union countries and its connection to their electoral turnout. The creation of the EU produced a civic education problem for its members. The citizens in these countries had to familiarize themselves with a new electoral system in addition to their existing electoral system. Using turnout as an evaluation tool for the education process, states have experienced mixed results.

When discussing civic education I utilize the Kenny, Logueny and Burban definition of voter education, which is defined as "education targeting voters (or a sub-set thereof) as such and linked to a specific education" (2001: 4). This is necessarily broad. Voter education is not simply including a pamphlet in the mail to all voters and hoping that they read and understand it, rather it needs a variety of programs to reach different groups of people and in different ways. Furthermore, I define citizen knowledge as having basic knowledge of the

Dr. Shauna Reilly is an Assistant Professor at Northern Kentucky University. She studies the impact of the public on institutions, primarily through public opinion and direct democracy election studies.

institutions (how to elect representatives, different aspects of the institution), and trust in those institutions (Milner 2002).[1]

The EU's electoral union was founded in 1992 and provides an excellent case to examine the civic education and its impact on electoral systems. The EU system, enacted in all member countries, was superimposed on all prior governmental organizations. Since, its inception the EU has experienced low turnout. During the 2004 election, the EU had 25 member countries and the lowest turnout in its history, only 45.3% of all eligible European voters participated (IFES). Furthermore, the turnout in nine of the fifteen member-countries prior to 2004 showed a downward trend in turnout (even in countries with mandatory elections) (Euroactiv). This is a disturbing trend – the EU is a relatively new electoral body and its turnout is already in decline, and citizens of new members are not participating in EU elections. Why is this turnout decreasing? Turnout is often used as a measure of civic attention and an evaluation of electoral systems (Milner 2002; Norris 2004) because participation requires at least acknowledgement of the system and when to vote. Can this decreasing turnout be reversed or even minimized by public education about the EU and its electoral system?

There were ten additional member states during the 2004 election from the previous election in 1999. Yet, the turnout in these countries was pitiful, as low as 16.7 percent in Slovakia; in fact, all but two of these new member states had turnout under 50 percent (Euroactiv). I suggest that this is because of the lack of education on the EU in these countries. They were admitted in 2004 just prior to the election; thus, their low turnout is not necessarily unexpected. Furthermore, there were no formal universal programs designed to educate these new states about the electoral system and citizens' role in this union.[2] However, future turnout should increase as citizens in these countries become more familiar with the electoral system and the EU itself.

Scholars have found a deficit in the number of programs, which educated citizens on the new electoral system. However, there are a host of programs that

---

[1] This includes trust because trusting an institution means that people know enough about the institution and trust that it will act and respond democratically.

[2] At the time of this research, there were no specific EU programs that sponsored civic education of the public after creation of the EU's electoral system even with direct contact with the EU. A European Commission report of voter education identified 157 projects since 1992 that related to voter education. Additionally, EuroAid has funded a variety of education programs on topics such as human rights, youth, support for the electoral processes, political education and rights, civil society, and support for the rule of law (Kenny, Logueny and Burban 2001: 5). These vast arrays of projects certainly have a connection to voter education but none succinctly outlined the civic education that scholars expect to find.

attempted to accomplish that goal by focusing on different aspects of citizenship (Kenny, Logueny and Burban 2001). However, this line of study was not completely futile. Some definitive problems were discovered that stood in the way of citizen education in the EU. These problems include lack of strategy, lack of monitoring and organizational learning; and lack of problem analysis (Kenny, Logueny and Burban 2001). It is truly difficult to educate the public with little direction, no follow up and no monitoring. Nonetheless, Europeans remain generally uninformed about the EU and have the negative perception that elites are administering EU (Tillman 2004). Therefore, previous attempts at civic education in the EU have not had lasting impacts on the knowledge of the citizenry nor on the trust levels of Europeans in the EU institution. Thus, the success of these programs cannot be celebrated but potentially be revised and revisited.

The European Parliament is seen as being an extension of national politics and national elections. Looking at turnout and citizen education, it is important to look at the state programs. There is a connection between the satisfaction levels with democracy in a voters own country and with the satisfaction with democracy in the EU (Blondel et al 1998: 77). The use of the 2005 Eurobarometer study included in this essay looks at citizen knowledge of the EU and satisfaction with democracy in order to evaluate this connection.

Of the EU member states, 22 have a proportional representation systems (France and Lithuanian have 2-round majoritarian systems; Great Britain has a first-past-the-post single-member parliamentary system). Therefore, the EU electoral system is not unfamiliar; however, with the multitude of elections and electoral systems it is important that the citizenry be educated on this additional electoral system. As prior research suggests, the institutional influence is minimal in the EU so there should be little decrease in voter turnout since people are already familiar with the electoral structure. This confirms earlier suggestions that the lack of knowledge surrounding the EU is causing this lack of participation, despite similarities in the electoral system.

There has been a variety of responses to joining the EU from member countries. While there are certain economic benefits, countries like Great Britain are reluctant to completely "Europeanize" and lose their independence. Other countries, specifically new members, have struggled to meet the requirements and believe that the costs associated with membership are minor to the benefits they will reap. The expectation is that these new member states want to be part of the EU and participate in all levels, yet their turnout rates are dismal.

The different systems and different reactions to the EU have, in part, led to different participation levels. Great Britain's electoral system is the most different from the EU system. Thus, it may be more difficult for them to convert to the new system because they already have different levels of authority and the addition of another may increase confusion and apathy. As discussed earlier there are differences in systems (such as list systems or two-round systems) that could result in different reactions to this new system. The difference in turnout may be related to the difference in the systems, which relates to political knowledge. The more dramatic the change, the more education is needed on behalf of the state to engage the population to participate in the new system.

Citizen education is a fundamental component to any democracy. Elections require participation (turnout) in order to function but also in order to have legitimacy. Electoral reform has many impetuses – election fraud, new states, evolution of the population, and the will of the people (Mann 2001). How do electoral reformers go about the process of educating the public on this new system? Mann discusses the importance of civic education and the government's role in it:

> Every level of government – national state and local – has a clear interest in developing and financing programs that educate citizens about their rights and responsibilities as voters. Registration instructions and confirmations, polling place locations and hours of operations, sample ballots, voter guides and voting equipment demonstrations should all be provided to citizens on a timely basis. Civic, educational, political and media organizations should do more to educate citizens on the nuts and bolts of voting. … By increasing knowledge about when, where, and how to vote, these educational efforts might have the fortunate side effect of engaging more citizens in the democratic process. (2001: 7).

Mann's eloquent passage shows the importance and necessity of voter education and how this is the responsibility of the state. The state(s) must take action on educating its public about electoral processes.

Civic literacy is a term used frequently in political science. Scholars have studied the notion of political literacy and have found that it is a "product of both internal motivations and abilities, and external social roles. Political literacy results from political involvement that is caused by social position, ability, and parental socialization" (Cassel and Lo 1997: 328). Therefore, civic literacy is something attained over a lifetime but it can be increased through school education and national/international education programs. Cassel and Lo find that education and political literacy are linked (1997; Milner 2002; Bowler and Donovan 1994). Education is vital to a healthy democracy and levels of participation.

Electoral reform is not without complications and restraints. The majority of electoral reform is done by individual states, building off existing electoral systems, and rarely involves a completely new electoral organism. The EU is exceptional in this way. While its member states had existing electoral systems, the EU added a layer of elections and complexity to member states. Several components of the EU system share similarities with member states – yet the addition of these elections adds complexity to the system. By creating additional elections and systems, there are more requirements of citizens. They have to turnout out to vote in a separate elections. They have to educate themselves on a different slate of issues and candidates. They still need to maintain their understanding of their current system.

Theory and Literature

This paper has a theoretical founding in the theories of participation and education. Motivation to participate in elections comes from a variety of individual influences such as costs and benefits, interest, and connectedness. However, knowledge about the process is a definitive explanation for participation. To understand the process and the institutions provides information on the ability to weigh costs and benefits.

Participation

Participation in elections is the foundation of democracy. When citizens do not participate in elections, they are not participating in democracy. Downsian models of democracy suggest that people should not vote because of the costs associated with it and the efficacy that the vote actually has (1957). Participation in elections does come at a cost, perhaps not as overtly as a poll tax, but there are time costs, education costs, and financial costs associated with the simple act of participation. Citizens need to take the time to actually vote, this means getting to the polls. There are also additional costs such as the cost of educating yourself on the issues/candidates involved in the election and the financial repercussion of taking the time off work to participate in elections (Rosenstone and Hansen 2003). This cost/benefit relationship cannot be ignored. Citizens tend to be free riders in terms of the electoral system so acknowledging extra efforts and costs to citizens is vital to understanding their turnout.

Contrary to Downs, a substantial number of people still participate in the electoral process. Why do people participate? Perhaps there is a civic duty that accounts for this voting (Niemi and Weisberg 1993). This civic duty can come from a sense of community and relationships with your community (Milner 2002; Putnam 2000). Connection with your community is an important consideration in terms of education and voting participation. Community involvement can lead to increased knowledge on aspects of the electoral system and the government as a whole just because of increased interactions with fellow citizens. Further, there is a connection of voting based on interactions with your community. Individuals are more likely to vote when those they are connected to also participate (Zuckerman 2005). Therefore, motivation to participate can come from a variety of sources.

Participation in elections has declined in the European Union since its inception. The decline has shocked and stumped many political leaders. The European Union is (at times) a controversial body that is expanding and growing to become a powerful force in the international world. Europeans who have the opportunity to participate should be turning out in droves to have their opinions heard. However, they are instead shunning the institution and its elections.

Nonvoting or nonparticipation can sometimes been seen as a form of voting itself. The choice not to participate can be a direct reflection of an individual's attitude toward the electoral process or the government itself (Sigelman 1982). While this is not measured traditionally as a type of voting behavior the meaning of it is not lost. In the EU, turnout has gradually declined; thus, the message of nonvoting as voting is somewhat less pronounced. Yet, scholars have to acknowledge that there are factors driving this nonvoting.

Mobilization is a significant challenge in the EU. Elections require turnout in addition to regular national elections. Mobilization can be increased through direct contact with citizens by a member of a political party or a political leader themselves (Rosenstone and Hansen 2003). Getting people out to the polls means that the election has to mean something to them. That meaning can only be achieved through civic education and political sophistication.

Voter Fatigue

Voter fatigue is another factor that drives down turnout in elections. Several elections that occur in a close proximity of time can create voter fatigue (Franklin 2003). These frequent elections create apathy on part of the population and thus, this can create lower turnout. This is particularly an issue in the EU. Member countries in the EU have multiple levels of elections (local, national and international) and they cannot help but feel overwhelmed. These multiple elections can lead to depressed turnout (Franklin 2003).

Satisfaction

To participate in the electoral system, the public must feel that there is some benefit from their participation. Part of this benefit is derived from how satisfied the public is with the institution. Public satisfaction with democracy in the EU is a consequence of the EU electoral system. Karp, Bowler and Banducci explore the reforms in the EU to counter concerns of democratic deficit (2003). They find that there are connections between satisfaction and knowledge; those who have higher levels of political knowledge are more likely to be satisfied with the democracy in the EU (Karp, Bowler and Banducci, 2003). The knowledge and democratic connection made by Karp, Bowler and Banducci has some long-term effects. Are institutions more responsive to those who know more about them? This provides a substantial democratic deficit that the state should seek to limit.

Integration

European integration has been a contentious issue in the EU (Aspinwall 2002). Referendums provide the government with insight into what the public wants in terms of policy, further integration, and a constitution. These referendums start with members of the European Community dating back to 1972. The direct elections and increase in powers of the European Parliament were supposed to increase the democratic component of the EU (Blondel et al 1998). Christin and Hug find that referendums increase citizen support for European integration (2002). This is surprising because of the previous findings that Europeans are generally uninformed about the issues surrounding the EU. I can only suggest that referendum campaigns increase civic education; thus, increasing citizen knowledge about the EU and the issues surrounding it. Christin and Hug add a caveat to their findings, by detailing the limitations of referendums and direct democracy and their impact on the public. They state, "simply holding a referendum on European integration does not necessarily increase the standing of the EU in the public's opinion" (2002: 606). Thus, institutions have little impact on opinions. Institutions can educate people to give them enough information to form their own opinions about these organization.

Education

Education does not simply stand by itself. Education as part of civic literacy leads to participation. Civic literacy is "education" that includes trust, political knowledge, media consumption as well as academic education (Milner 2002). Education in this combination is essential to a new democracy – be it a developing country or a supranational organization.

Participation and education are interrelated. The more educated a population is the more likely they are to participate politically. This education can include a variety of types, such as political knowledge, formal education and debate or interactions about politics. Citizens with more formal education are more likely to participate in elections (Rosenstone and Hansen 2003; Verba and

Nie 1972; Lane 1959). Citizens can also gain political sophistication through interactions in their community. Thus, older citizens will have more interactions, knowledge and skills and be more prepared to participate in their electoral system (Rosenstone and Hansen 2003).

Electoral Engineering
        The design of an electoral system is a complex task that considers numerous factors. When looking at the turnout of elections and education it is important to see how the design of these processes influences the outcomes of elections. Previous research on electoral engineering has focused on the type of electoral system at the level of turnout (Norris 2004). Thus, there must be systemic influences on issues like turnout from the type of electoral system. Norris (2004) qualifies turnout as a product of the electoral system whereas I posit that turnout can be used as a tool for evaluating the electoral system. Using turnout as an evaluation tool in the EU system would allow us to look at cultural influences, such as civic education, to see what influence this has on electoral turnout. Since the EU is a proportional representation system and relatively young, we can expect two things: one that it will have relatively high turnout and two, as this democracy "ages", its turnout will increase. However, as noted above, this is not true for the EU, it has burgeoning voter decline. Perhaps the missing variable in this story is the lack of education on the EU electoral system to the mass public.

Hypotheses
        Based on previous research and on the exploration of this essay, I have defined several hypotheses. The primary hypothesis of this paper is that knowledge about the EU is an important component in determining variations in voter turnout in EU. Higher levels of political knowledge and higher satisfaction with the EU lead to higher political turnout in EU Parliamentary elections. The second hypothesis identifies a relationship between proximity of national and EU elections. The closer a state's elections are to the elections of the EU the lower the turnout for the EU election.

Methods and Data
        This paper uses the 2005 Eurobarometer to explore civic knowledge in the EU. The Eurobarometer does not include any turnout variables; therefore, I aggregated the Eurobarometer data to create a new data set by country (these aggregations are detailed throughout the paper). A turnout percentage for the 2004 election was included in this data set for each country. The unit of analysis

for this study is the aggregated measures for individual countries not their individual citizens.

Main variables included in this study of knowledge in the EU are trust in institutions (national government and the EU); support for the EU, enlargement and the constitution; and self reported knowledge of the EU. To further examine the knowledge of the EU, indicators such as questions about the number of members, when the EU elections are, how members of the European Parliament are elected and whether the EU has an anthem, are used.

Respondents were asked how knowledgeable they felt about the European Union in the Eurobarometer as part of the Knowledge variable. They were asked on a 0 to 9 scale; 0 being no knowledge and 9 being a great deal of knowledge. The number of respondents in each state who answered at each level are multiplied by the number associated with their response. These responses are aggregated in each state and divided by the total number of respondents for that state to create a knowledge score for each country.

There are measures for support of the constitution, favor a political union, support for enlargement, and trust in national and EU governments are the percentages of a state population who support these issues respectively. They are derived by taking the number of supporters and dividing it by the total number of respondents for each country.

Turnout variables for 2004 and 1999 are collected from the Euroactiv article. These percentages of turnout are provided for each of the 25 countries included in this study. In 1999, there were only 15 members of the EU and only these member states voted in the European Parliament's election.

The variables: know Members, know when Elections, know how to elect EP and know anthem come from questions about true/false questions asked in the Eurobarometer questionnaire. The true or false answers, which were correct, are coded as yes and all other responses no. These answers are aggregated to state level data and into a percentage of the state population who answered correctly.

Likewise, satisfaction with democracy is a score that is created by multiplying the number of respondents unsatisfied with democracy by -1 and those who were satisfied by 1 and aggregating these variables to create a satisfaction measure per state.

Table 1: 2004 Turnout Regression of Knowledge Variables

	Coefficient	SE	T
Knowledge	-8.74	8.61	-1.01
Support Constitution	30.61	36.87	.83
Satisfied with Democracy	.199**	.087	2.29
Support Enlargement	-104.90**	28.83	-3.64
Favor Political Union	29.09	54.74	.53
Trust National government	-.985	18.76	-.01
Trust EU Government	-1.07	71.23	-.01
Know Members	-32.33	31.2	-1.04
Know When Elections Are	-31.04	41.38	-.75
Know How to Elect EP	100.90**	35.41	2.85
Know Anthem	7.08	21.86	.32
	80.46	46.12	1.74

** p < .05   * p < .1
N=25 R^2=.7566**

Looking at the 2004 election, in Table 1, the model explains 76% of the variation in turnout. With this election (post expansion of the EU), we see that those states who are satisfied with democracy and know how the European Parliament Members are elected are likely to have a higher turnout. A significant finding in this model is that those countries with higher percentages of the population who know how to elect the EU increases turnout for that election. Further, those states that are satisfied with democracy and favor a political union in the EU are going to have higher turnout in EU elections. Surprisingly, support for enlargement has a negative impact on turnout. Other factors that decrease turnout include trust in either the EU or national governments. While these negative findings are unexpected there are also some indicators that knowledge (knowing members and when they are elected) decreases turnout.

Control variables of *Catholic* and *ideology* are used in this analysis. The percentage of catholic population in the state can affect its acceptance/ participation in EU elections because of the connection with the institution of the Catholic Church. These responses were aggregated into percentages for each of the countries in this study. Further, a country's ideological position can affect their support for integration/participation in the EU (Aspinwall 2002). The *ideological* variable is measured by multiplying the number of left respondents by -1 and right respondents by 1. These are then aggregated to create an ideological measure for the state.

Another control variable is used to investigate the impact of new members and knowledge in European elections. *Previous members* is calculated by looking at which countries were members prior to the 1999 election. The 2004 election is remarkable because of the large number of states who were new members. Thus, previous members are expected to have higher turnout because they are more knowledgeable and have more experience about European Union elections. Further, because of ballot fatigue, I have added a variable to account for the *proximity of the recent election* in a given country.

Table 2 – Country Elections and EU Turnout

Country	Election Years	EU Turnout %
Austria	2006/2002	49.4/41.8
Belgium	2003/1999	91.0/90.8
Cyprus	2006/2001	71.2
Czech	2006/2002	27.9
Denmark	2005/2001	47.8/50.5
Estonia	2003/1999	26.9
Finland	2003/1999	41.1/31.4
France	2002/1997	43.1/46.8
Germany	2005/2002	43.0/45.2
Great Britain	2005/2001	38.9/24
Greece	2004/2000	62.8/75.3
Hungary	2006/2002	38.5
Ireland	2002/1997	59.7/50.2
Italy	2006/2001	73.1/70.8
Latvia	2006/2002	41.2
Lithuania	2004/2000	48.2
Luxemburg	2004/1999	90.0/87.3
Malta	2003/1998	82.4
Netherlands	2006/2003	39.1/30
Poland	2005/2001	20.4
Portugal	2005/2002	38.7/40
Slovakia	2006/2002	16.7
Slovenia	2004/2000	28.3
Spain	2004/2000	45.9/63
Sweden	2006/2002	37.2/38.8

Source: Euroactiv and Elections and Parties in Europe

Table 2 provides several insights; first, the differences in electoral systems. It is important to note the three countries with non-Proportional Representation systems (namely Great Britain, France and Lithuania) have some of the lower numbers of turnout, with none having more than 50% of their population turn out for the European Parliament elections in 1999 or 2004. In addition, Great Britain, whose electoral system is the most different from the European Parliament's, had the lowest turnout of all member states in 1999. This is important because it shows the lack of familiarity about the political system can result in a decrease in participation.

Second, Table 2 demonstrates that the frequency of elections is often a concern for voter turnout and this is especially true when superimposing a second type of government on another system. The frequency or closeness of the EU and national elections is addressed in both Table 1 and Table 2. For example: Spain, Greece, Poland, Estonia, Slovenia and Lithuania all have elections within one year of the EU elections and the EU turnout for these countries is extremely low. Further, Spain and Greece had been members of the EU for both the 1999 and 2004 election. They had national elections in close proximity to the EU elections and their turnout for the second election decreased substantially from the first election. Thus, the proximity of national and EU elections does have an impact. However, I should also note that in Luxembourg elections were held in 1999 and 2004, the same years as EU elections, yet, their turnout is hovering at 90 percent. The closer the national election is to the European Union elections, it is expected that these voters will have higher fatigue and participate less. Therefore, this variable represents the years since the last national election.

Table 3: EU 2004 Turnout Regression with Controls

	Coefficient	SE	T
Knowledge	-11.14	12.73	-.88
Support Constitution	30.55	54.84	.56
Satisfied with Democracy	.311**	.101	3.08
Support Enlargement	-125.92	74.24	-1.70
Favor Political Union	73.88	100.94	.73
Trust National Government	3.34	28.15	.12
Trust EU Government	-79.9	104.49	-.76
Know When Elections	-15.32	72.29	-.21
Know How to Elect EP	92.78	49.52	1.87
Know Anthem	3.74	40.16	.09
Ideology	-.012	.178	-.16

Table 3: EU 2004 Turnout Regression with Controls (continued)

	Coefficient	SE	T
Catholic	-2.89	21.67	-.13
Previous Members	-5.08	19.64	-.26
Proximity of Country Elections	120.4	99.53	1.21

** $p < .05$ * $p < .1$
N=25 R^2=.7874**

The addition of controls and previous members to the regression results in an increase in the explanatory value of the model but it results in fewer significant variables. The addition of these variables does support that when there is a larger percentage of Catholic population in a specific country, there will be a related lower voting turnout of that country's population.   Additionally, members prior to the 2004 expansion have a decreased turnout in the EU elections. This is consistent with the findings in Table 1. Further, these findings support earlier discussion that turnout is declining in the EU. However, it is surprising that the countries who have been exposed to the EU longer do not have higher turnout, as they would be more educated (due to longevity in the Union) about the organization. Nonetheless, turnout in the new countries could be higher because of recent admittance and potentially more recent exposure to the workings of the EU electoral system. What was expected was that because the new member countries were admitted just prior to the 2004 election that there would be little difference in the turnouts of these groups.

An interesting and important finding of Table 3 is that proximity of national elections has a positive impact on turnout; thus, the more years between the previous national election and the EU election, the higher the turnout for individual countries. This is important because it demonstrates that the findings tells election planners that election fatigue is an important consideration in the EU electoral turnout.

Conclusion

This research has shown that there is a connection between education/ knowledge and electoral turnout. When looking at the process of electoral engineering or changing systems, an important consideration is educating the public on the new system. This process of education must include education on the electoral system but also of the governmental body itself. Further, understanding the system is just one component of this research. Trust is another important component of this education. Institutions need to instill confidence in the population. This trust and confidence is necessary to provide programs to the state but also in order to get the population to support them. While trust is insignificant and in the opposite direction than expected, the relationship between trust in the EU and voter turnout needs further investigation to completely understand what is going on and if there is something that is not being addressed through that variable.

When discussing the turnout for the EU it is important to note that the closeness of national elections to the EU elections can affect turnout. Luxembourg is the exception to the case; however, other EU countries demonstrate voter fatigue when there are multiple elections in close proximity to one another. Furthermore, new member states are not the only EU countries with low turnout, previous members of the EU have experienced decline in turnout. The EU needs to address this issue in order to maintain the legitimacy of this organization.

The EU needs to consider several things if they hope to achieve higher turnout for their elections. First, they need to build trust in the institution. Second, they must listen to the public desires on expansion of the EU and on the EU Constitution – the failure of the EU to be responsive to the public has created distrust and disdain for the organization, which has resulted in lower turnout. Third, the EU needs to be mindful of national elections and have EU elections when they are least affected by national elections to limit voter fatigue. Finally, and most importantly, the EU needs to educate its citizens on the EU itself. Increased citizen education on the EU can only lead to increased turnout and trust in the EU.

Future Research

This study is limited because it is looking at individual countries as the unit of analysis and at a superimposed governmental system. Future research in the area of political knowledge and electoral turnout in new systems could be explored at the individual level. Being able to measure individual turnout and individual knowledge levels could only strengthen the importance of this research. Another fruitful area of research could focus on the individual state governments and the impact of their domestic situation on the political knowledge of the European Union.

References

Aspinwall, Mark. 2002. "Preferring Europe: Ideology and National Preferences on European Integration" *European Union Politics,* Vol. 3, No. 1, 81-111.

Birzea, Cesar. "European Citizenship as a Cultural and Political Construct" http://www.jsse.org/2005-se/birzea_european_citizenship.htm

Blondel, Jean, Richard Sinnott and Palle Svensson. 1998. *People and Parliament in the European Union: Participation, Democracy and Legitimacy.* Oxford: Clarendon Press.

Bowler, Shaun and Todd Donovan. 1994. "Information and Opinion Change on Ballot Propositions" *Political Behavior*, v. 16, n. 4: 411-35.

Cassel, Carol A. and Celia C. Lo. 1997. "Theories of Political Literacy" *Behavioral Science* 19 (4): 317-335.

Christin, Thomas and Simon Hug. 2002. "Referendums and Citizens Support for European Integration" *Comparative Political Studies* v. 35, n.5, 586-617.

Downs, Anthony. 1957. *An Economic Theory of Democracy*. New York: Harper.

Euroactive, "Voter turnout 1979 and 2004 in the EU-15" Nov. 4, 2006. http://www.euractiv.com/en/elections/european-parliament-elections-2004-results/article-117482

Farrell, David M. and Roger Scully. 2002 "Electoral System Effects on Parliamentary Representation: The Case of the European Parliament" prepared for the American Political Science Association meeting August 29 – September 1, 2002. Nov 1, 2006 http://www.meps.org.uk/mepwebsite/Farrell_Scully_paper.pdf

Fowler, Linda, Pieter L. Polhuis, and Scott C. Paine. 1983. "Changing Patterns of Voting Strength in the European Parliament" *Comparative Politics*, v. 15, n. 2. p. 159-175.

Franklin, Jane. 2003. "Social Capital: Policy and Politics" *Social Policy and Society* 2(4): 349-352.

IFES "European Union Election Guide" Nov. 4, 2006 http://www.electionguide.org/country-news.php?ID=244

Karp, Jeffrey A., Shaun Bowler and Susan A. Banducci (2003) 'Electoral Systems, Party Mobilization, and Turnout. Evidence from the European Parliamentary Elections', *British Elections and Parties Review* 13.

Kenny, Karen, Sophie Lagueny and Florence Burban. 2001 "Evaluation of Voter Education in the Context of EU Electoral Support" Nov 2, 2006 http://ec.europa.eu/comm/europeaid/evaluation/reports/sector/951598_final.pdf

Lane, Robert E. 1959. *Political Life: Why and How People Get Involved in Politics*. New York: Free Press.

Lehoucq, Fabrice Edouard. 2000. "Institutionalizing Democracy: Constraint and Ambition in the Politics of Electoral Reform" *Comparative Politics* 32 (4): 459-477.

Mann, Thomas E. 2001. "An Agenda for Election Reform" Brooking Policy Brief Series, Paper #82. http://www.brookings.edu/research/papers/2001/06/elections-mann

Milner, Henry. 2002. *Civic Literacy: How Informed Citizens Make Democracy Work*. Hanover, NH: University Press of New England.

Niemi, Richard G. and Herbert F. Weisberg. 1993. "Is it Rational To Vote?" in *Classics in Voting Behavior* eds. Richard Niemi and Herbert Weisberg. Washington: Congressional Quarterly Press.

Norris, Pippa. 2004. *Electoral Engineering: Voting Rules and Political Behavior*. New York: Cambridge University Press.

Papacostas, Antonis. *Eurobaromter 63.4: European Union Enlargement, the European Constitution, Economic Challenges ,Innovative Products and Services*. May-June 2005 [Computer file]. ICPSR04564-v1. London, England: TNS Opinion & Social [producer], 2005. Cologne, Germany: Zentralarchiv fur Empirische Sozialforschung/Ann Arbor, MI: Inter-university Consortium for Political and Social Research [distributors], 2006-10-19.

Parties and Elections In Europe, November 26, 2006 http://www.parties-and-elections.de/countries.html

Putnam, Robert D. 2000 *Bowling Alone: The Collapse and Revival of American Community*. New York: Simon & Schuster

Rose, Richard. "Voter Turnout in the European Union Member Countries'" in Voter Turnout in Western Europe from the International Institute for Democracy and Electoral Assistance Website. Nov 2, 2006 http://www.idea.int/publications/voter_turnout_weurope/ upload/ Chapter%202.pdf

Rosenstone, Steven J. and John Mark Hansen. 2003. *Mobilization, Participation, and Democracy in America.* New York: Pearson Education, Inc.

Sigelman, Lee. 1982. "The Nonvoting Voter in Voting Research" *American Journal of Political Science* 26 (1): 47-56

Thomassen, Jacques and Hermann Schmitt. 1999. "In Conclusion: Political Representation and Legitimacy in the European Union" in *Political Representation and Legitimacy in the European Union.* Eds. Hermann Schmitt and Jacques Thomassen. New York: Oxford University Press.

Tillman, Erik R. "The European Union at the Ballot Box? European Integration and Voting Behavior in the New Member States" *Comparative Political Studies* v. 37, n. 5, 590-610.

Verba, Sidney and Norman H. Nie. 1972. *Participation in America: Political Democracy and Social Equality* New York: Harper and Row.

Zuckerman, Alan S. ed. 2005. *The Social Logic of Politics: Personal Networks as Contexts for Political Behavior.* Philadelphia: Temple University Press.

BEST PRACTICES:
PROCESS EVALUATION OF A DIVERSION PROGRAM

Jennifer L. Huck
Carroll University

Kendra N. Bowen
Tarleton State University

This article highlights the findings of a process evaluation of Justice 2000, Inc. Treatment and Diversion Program (TAD). This evaluation surveyed all TAD employees, including case managers and supervisors. The purpose of this study was to examine the implementation and fidelity of TAD based upon pretrial diversion standards developed in 1995 by the National Association of Pretrial Service Agencies (NAPSA) as well as self-identified outcome goals. Justice 2000 identifies the NAPSA standards as providing the foundational underpinnings of TAD from its conception to implementation. TAD began its operation in Milwaukee County in 2007 with the aid of state funding. It operates in conjunction with other programs of Justice 2000, Inc., the public defender's office, the district attorney's office, and private attorneys. The findings herein are exploratory in nature and best understood in combination with other evaluations of best practice approaches.

The number of individuals in the criminal justice system has risen significantly since the inception of the war on drugs, now totaling over two million (The GAINS Center, 1997; Mauer, 2001). A number of these drug offenders under criminal justice supervision have a range of other concerns and issues including substance abuse and/or mental health concerns (Abram & Teplin, 1991; Steadman, Osher, Robbins, Case, & Samuels, 2009). Despite the growing number of individuals incarcerated with substance abuse problems, there are a limited number of treatment programs and other resources available (Staton-Tindall, Havens, Oser, Prendergast, & Leukefeld, 2009). More than 80% of incarcerated individuals are substance users; however, only half of those receive any type of substance abuse treatment while incarcerated (The U.S. Department of Justice, Office of Justice Programs, Bureau of Justice Statistics, 2006). Now more than ever, there is a dire need for diversion and release programs to relieve pressure from prisons. Subsequently, it is important to ensure diversion and release programs are successful in diverting individuals from the criminal justice system.

Coinciding with the war on drugs, various diversion and release programs were implemented throughout the United States with the common goals of

Jennifer L. Huck is an assistant professor of criminal justice/sociology for Carroll University. Her research interests include theoretical criminology, courtroom decision-making, and criminal justice programming.

Kendra N. Bowen is an assistant professor of criminal justice for Tarleton State University. Her research interests include violence and victimology, theoretical criminology, and policy.

reducing jail and prison populations as well as the stigma from court processes (see, Ogloff, Roesch, & Hart, 1994; Steadman, & Naples, 2005). Pretrial release programs remove charged defendants from jail who have yet to be adjudicated. Pretrial release programs place stipulations on the individual, such as involvement in a monitoring program or entrance into a substance abuse treatment facility, for the ability to return to the community. An additional objective of diversion and release programs is to have the original charges lessened or dismissed upon successful completion of stipulations.

What is lacking in research of pretrial diversion programs is the systemic analysis of what works to identify best practices (Topics in Community Corrections, 2008; The Crime and Justice Institute and the National Institute of Corrections, 2007). Additionally, research should examine the programs' ability to protect defendants' legal rights by ensuring pretrial programs do not overreach their duties while maintaining integrity during program implementation and operation (Hankey, 2008; The Crime and Justice Institute and the National Institute of Corrections, 2007). Researchers must use clearly defined objectives and a framework to examine what pretrial programs are effective and what elements create success (Clark, 2008; Green, Smith, & Bryant, 2008). This evaluation completed in 2009 of the Justice 2000, Inc. Treatment and Diversion Program (TAD), started in Milwaukee County in 2007, aids the best practices literature of pretrial diversion programs for defendants who have substance abuse concerns.

TAD's foundation lies in NAPSA (National Association of Pretrial Service Agencies) standards and additional self-identified outcome goals. NAPSA is a national non-profit organization based in Wisconsin that provides standards and advocates for pretrial programs. NAPSA's original protocols were created in 1978 and updated in 1995 to include six main principles of pretrial services. According to these standards, pretrial diversion programs must (1) offer persons charged with criminal offenses alternatives to traditional criminal justice or juvenile justice proceedings; (2) permit participation by the accused only on a voluntary basis; (3) provide the accused access to defense counsel prior to a decision to participate; (4) occurs no sooner than the filing of formal charges and no later than a final adjudication of guilt; (5) develop service plans in conjunction with the defendant, which addresses the needs of that defendant and are structured to assist that person in avoiding behavior likely to lead to future arrests; and (6) result in dismissal of charges or its equivalent, if the divertee successfully completes the diversion process (National Association for Pretrial Services Agencies, 1995).

In addition to the NAPSA standards, TAD operates amid three outcome goals. These goals are (1) to divert people in need of substance abuse services from the criminal justice process into community based social and treatment services, (2) to reduce the number of people in need who have substance abuse services in the Milwaukee County Jail, and (3) to reduce the number of substance abusing defendants sent into the state prison system from Milwaukee County. This process evaluation studied the TAD program through its implementation integrity of the NAPSA standards and program outcome goals.

Method

The TAD program has a small number of employees ($N = 11$) who each contain vital information regarding program fidelity. Surveys were deemed a reliable tool to obtain data from the respondents/employees; logistical concerns and limited resources developed a need to complete surveys through electronic mail. To ensure a high response rate, the evaluation study was completed with the Dillman Tailored Design (Dillman, 2007). According to this method, potential participants are more likely to respond through multiple contacts including an introductory letter, survey distribution, reminder letter, survey redistribution, and a final unique contact. Due to a low response rate, contacts were increased from five to eight with an ending sample of seven respondents.

The survey included 58 closed-ended questions and eight open-ended questions (see Appendix A). The respondents received the survey via an email attachment and were requested to fill out the survey and return it to researchers as an email attachment. It was assured that the study was separate from Justice 2000 and that responses would not be connected to individuals as only aggregated responses would be reported. Due to the limited number of individuals in the sample (n=7), with one respondent not completing the survey, descriptive statistics were used to analyze the closed-ended responses. The open-ended responses were used to formulate stronger conclusions about the meaning of the descriptive statistics.

Findings

Overall, employees perceived TAD as being effective in applying the NAPSA standards and the goals. TAD seemingly implemented the program and client standards of best practice successfully; however, concerns do exist. Of highest concern, was TAD's inability to help more individuals due to limitations of resources including work force, access to treatment, and funding. In addition, employees spoke of limited community and criminal justice connections in that these entities are unsure of what TAD offers and what its clientele needs. Finally, employees expressed a need to make timelier decisions. The specifics of these findings are discussed in the following sections of Goals, Program Implementation – Program-Centered, and Program Implementation – Client-Centered.

Goals

The outcome goals have mixed support about the actualization of TAD's objectives (see Table 1). The first goal of diverting people in need of substance abuse services from the criminal justice process into community based social and treatment services contained the most discrepancy. This goal was addressed through two items, the first dealing with social services and the second with treatment services. Respondents concurred that clients were placed appropriately into social services but respondents disagreed that clients were connected properly to treatment services. The second and third goals of lowering the number of individuals with substance abuse concerns in Milwaukee County Jails and Wisconsin State Prison system were perceived by respondents as being met.

Table 1: Goals of TAD

Goal	Agree (*n*)	Disagree (*n*)
Social Services	3	4
Treatment Services	4	3
Milwaukee County Jail	7	0
Wisconsin State Prison	6	1

Program Implementation – Program-Centered

Program implementation measured if the program operated in the manner set forth by NAPSA pretrial diversion standards. These standards include categories of staff, collaboration, screening, program, service plan, funding, and community connection Overall, TAD employees perceived the program operating in a manner that is supportable by NAPSA standards; however, it is important to note that respondents varied in opinion within each of the categories, indicating that improvements in the fidelity of program implement-tation can be achieved.

The findings for the seven program-centered standards can be found in Table 2. *Staff* standards included education, training, diversity, and adequacy of employees. Although overall staff standards were viewed positively, concerns existed. Education and training components were adhered to by the TAD program; employees perceived that they have a proper amount of education and training, but red flags were raised as to the number of employees and the ease of burnout. Discussions with supervisors provided information that all employees have a bachelor's degree and that turnover is a concern in this program, similar to many social service agencies. In addition, respondents perceived that the employees do not reflect the diversity of the clientele; thus, the perception that clients were unable to connect to staff. Per program records, the majority of the staff are female (72%), white (61%), and educated (bachelor's degree) whereas program clients have a high-school diploma (26.9%) or less (41.7%) and are non-white (57.5%) and male (78.5%). The most similar quality between the employees and clientele would be age; 65.1% of clients and almost all employees (95.5%) were under the age of 30.

Table 2: Program Implementation – Program-Centered

Standard	Possible Range	Midpoint	Sample Range	Mean	Median	$(n) \geq$ Midpoint
Staff $\alpha = .844$	8 – 32	20	14 – 24	20.43	22	5
Collaboration $\alpha = .967$	4 – 16	10	4 – 14	9.71	9	3
Screening $\alpha = .651$	6 – 24	15	12 – 21	17.71	18	6
Program $\alpha = .787$	7 – 28	17.5	12 – 23	17.29	17	3
Service Plan $\alpha = .688$	8 – 32	20	19 – 29	23.00	23	6
Funding $\alpha = $ n/a	1 – 4	2	1-2	1.14	1	0
Community $\alpha = $ n/a	1 – 4	2	3 – 4	3.14	3	7

Collaboration is the degree to which employees of TAD, including case managers, supervisors, and management, work together as a cohesive unit. Employees viewed collaboration as a problem. Respondents do not believe that employees' opinions were sought when determining goals and objectives of the program, and that supervisors and managers have not examined client successes and failures for the betterment of TAD. The only positive collaboration item was that management was connected and concerned to employee-identified concerns.

Screening items determined the ability of TAD to adequately interview, assess, and make decisions about potential clients. Overall, no problems were identified in this NAPSA standard. Employees agreed that clients were assessed for social support, and that risks and criteria were equitably and consistently applied. However, respondents were concerned with the timeliness of decisions to accept or not accept potential clients, which is made by staff, supervisors and judges.

Both *program* and *service plan* concern the NAPSA standards focused upon the client, and whether the program operates in a manner that places clients' needs first and foremost. Service plans were supported and perceived as being an effective component of TAD; however, minor disagreement existed when questioned if service plans were flexible and placed the client as an integral part of the service plan creation. Respondents did agree, however, that collaboration existed during the creation of service to maximize the individual needs, risks, and goals to create a more crime-free lifestyle. Program elements were viewed as needing improvement as only 3 responders were above the midpoint for the scale. With respect to programs, the concerns exist because employees did not believe TAD had the ability to provide necessary resources due to access and availability of programs; it appears that the program measures connected to TAD such as providing assessments, identifying need, and reaching appropriate clients are working properly. It is arguable that most concerns do not reside inside TAD but in the ability of TAD to find, access, and connect to appropriate outside community resources within budgetary constraints.

These findings are emphasized when connected to the *community* and *funding* categories. All respondents perceived TAD as having a positive connection and relationship with community resources. Yet, funding was a major concern and not one respondent believed that funding was at an adequate amount to operate TAD properly and fulfill the needs of its clientele.

Program Implementation – Client-Centered

Client-centered program implementation measurement was constructed with 17 items about the connection of the client to TAD program including determinants of success, coercion, and relay of information. These items were answered through a likert scale of never, sometimes, usually, and always. The total possible range was 18 to 72 with a midpoint of 44. The respondent sample range was 39 to 55 with four respondents above the midpoint to indicate the client-centered standards were implemented adequately, but again on the lower side suggesting fidelity could be strengthened.

Of the three client-centered standards, *relay of information* was the only one viewed consistently positive. Specifically, respondents stated clients receive proper information before making a decision about entering TAD, defense counsel was used and helpful in making this decision, and individual client characteristics (e.g., disabilities) were taken into consideration when employees explained TAD to potential clients.

Unfortunately, concerns were identified with both determinants of success and coercion. With respect to *determinants of success*, the majority of respondents believed that staff, clients, and the criminal justice system could do more to ensure a successful completion of the program (see Table 3). The possible range of responses was 3 to 12 with the majority being at a score of seven, which lies between sometimes and usually. Importantly, when respondents were asked if clients were successful in completing TAD, the only responses selected were usually and sometimes. Thus, clients are perceived as being successful but the prevailing perception of the participants was that the program and criminal justice system could do more to ensure client success.

Table 3: Determinants of Success

Who can do more ...	Never (*n*)	Sometimes (*n*)	Usually (*n*)	Always (*n*)
Staff	0	2	5	0
Clients	0	3	3	1
Criminal Justice System	0	3	4	0

Lastly, coercion has mixed results (see Table 4). It is important to note that all respondents indicated clients enter the program voluntarily with the majority of responses in the usually and always category. All respondents, however, stated coercion existed either with staff, public defender, and/or the system. Further, the majority of responses fell in the usually and always categories, indicating that coercion might be a major concern for TAD. These results need more exploration to justify a strong conclusion, including information about what type of coercion is used and how it is harmful to participants.

Table 4: Coercion

Origin of Coercion	Never (*n*)	Sometimes (*n*)	Usually (*n*)	Always (*n*)
Staff	1	1	2	3
Defense Attorney	1	1	4	1
Criminal Justice System	0	0	2	5
Voluntary Involvement?	0	2	2	3

Open-Ended Questions

Respondents were asked a series of open-ended questions used to draw conclusions and provide a foundation for the evaluation. General conclusions reached concerned what characteristics employees perceived as making a client successful and how the community and the criminal justice system connections could be improved (see Figure 1). Employees suggested that collaboration was instrumental to clients' success as well as the client being amenable to treatment and TAD. Further, connections with the community and criminal justice system could be strengthened if training and education were offered to provide information about TAD and the full spectrum of clients' needs. Lastly, community and criminal justice connections were referred to as necessary for the success of TAD and its clientele but increased success may be reached if inter-organizational communication were improved.

Figure 1: Main Themes Selected From the Open-Ended Responses.

What can make a client successful?
• Stable living situation
• Source of income
• Strong community connection
• Strong support system
• Proper assessment and service plan
• Desire for treatment
• Access to treatment
• Amenable to treatment services
How can community connections be improved?
• Funding
• Training and education
• Field visits to resources
• Staff must build awareness of programs
• Maintaining contact in a changing environment
How can criminal justice connections be improved?
• Funding
• Training and education
• Job shadow
• Improved communication

Discussion

Process evaluations are crucial to the success of diversion and release programs (see, Newcomer, Hatry, & Wholey, 1994; Scheirer, 1994; Weiss, 1972). There are many advantages to evaluating these programs. First, it adds to the ever growing literature of evidence-based research, which helps researchers and practitioners alike to show what and how other programs have been successful. Second, if programs are not working, steps can be taken to change aspects of the program or to cease funding a non-working program. Lastly, if programs work, individuals are diverted successfully from an already overcrowded jail or prison system; this reduces strain on the system and increases the likelihood of success for these individuals in the future.

As with any evaluation, there are limitations to this study that cannot be overlooked. First, the sample size ($n = 7$) was small, however, this could not be avoided due to the small amount of employees that represent TAD ($N = 11$). The response rate (72%) was high and can be attributed to the Dillman Tailor Design Method. This study adds to the literature about the successfulness of the Dillman method, even though the means of distribution (i.e., electronic mail) is inconclusive of its appropriateness. Additionally, results might have been impacted due to the increased number of contacts used to obtain more (i.e., enough) responses. Yet, the majority of responses were received after the seventh contact to suggest that responses would be uniformly biased. Second, due to the small sample size, descriptive statistics could only be used. The statistical findings are meant to provide a better understanding of the data, but cannot be used to infer significance or be generalizable. Instead, the best use of these findings might be to aid programs in understanding the need to incorporate best practice standards in program implementation and to build process evaluations into program evaluations. A final limitation is that this study only examines viewpoints of TAD employees and not others involved with the program (i.e., courtroom actors and clients). The original study included a site visit and distribution of surveys to public defenders, district attorneys, and judges. A site visit did not occur due to logistical concerns including that the program became involved with state budget review hearings. The courtroom actor surveys were attempted but not enough surveys were returned for conclusions to be drawn.

Even with these limitations, the following conclusions can be surmised. In both the closed- and open-ended questions, respondents placed funding as a major concern for all aspects of the program. Many respondents believed that if funding were increased, TAD could be improved by hiring more employees, building stronger community relations, and training criminal justice system staff to understand the needs of clientele. Further, respondents were concerned with the lack of diversity among TAD employees. In the future, TAD could hire more employees that represent the diversity of TAD clientele or increase diversity and cultural awareness training. Community relations could be improved by ensuring the community is aware of TAD and its objectives, as well as the success of the program. These solutions would inevitably increase the effectiveness of TAD and the amount of individuals it could assist. In addition, collaboration between case managers, supervisors, and management must be improved to strengthen TAD. The open-ended questions demonstrated that case managers, as the employees with the greatest connections to clients, have invaluable information that should be sought and used for the benefit of TAD.

Based on employees' responses, the implementation and fidelity of TAD as defined by the 1995 NAPSA pretrial diversion standards has been mostly successful. Of utmost concern is standard two, participation on a voluntary basis. Although all respondents felt that clientele enter the program on a voluntary basis, all expressed concern with coercion. This topic needs to be explored further by TAD and Justice 2000, Inc. to determine what parts of the process are corrosive and what solutions exist. This coercion concern cannot be limited to only investigating staff, it is important that criminal justice system agents are included in the exploration to benefit clientele and the program. Also of concern, is standard six, the case will be dismissed or charges lessened. The survey had two items specifically addressing this standard and findings were inconclusive. Seemingly, employees were unsure of how to respond to these questions and some respondents typed that the questions were not appropriate because the conclusion of the case is dependent on its individual circumstances. In addition, an outcome evaluation might be more appropriate to determine if standard six is being met.

Overall, TAD was perceived as being effective in reducing the numbers of individuals with substance abuse concerns from the Milwaukee County Jail and Wisconsin State Prison System. The Population Health Institute of the University of Wisconsin (2008) found that as of August 2008, no TAD graduates were placed into the Wisconsin state prison system and on average 95 days of incarceration were avoided by TAD clients, which increased to 128 if they completed the program successfully. Additionally, as of August 2008, after approximately one year of operation, TAD saved 37,989 days of incarceration. Subsequently, it appears that the concerns with TAD did not rest in the program's connection to its goals and standards or the clients being unsuccessful but with the effectiveness of TAD in completing its duties with assessable resources. It is suggested that TAD remain a foundational component of the Milwaukee County criminal justice system to continue its aid to those clients needing diversion from incarceration.

Although the specific findings cannot be generalized to other pretrial diversion programs, the findings can aid programs as well as future research interests. It is the researchers' contention that the success of TAD lies with its foundational underpinnings and connection to a best practice approach. Other pretrial diversion programs should determine if NAPSA standards are appropriate for their program and perhaps evaluate the program using these as a fidelity measure. Future research must be able to take all aspects of a program into account prior to its evaluation and examine it at all crucial points (e.g., survey employees and courtroom actors). Additionally, outcome evaluations should be completed to ensure that both the process and outcomes are being actualized. For this evaluation, researchers felt that an outcome evaluation did not need to be completed. The Population Health Institute of the University of Wisconsin examined the outcome goals to conclude that TAD decreased prison and jail admissions of those with substance abuse concerns and reduces risk of recidivism.

In summation, TAD has adhered to the NAPSA standards of 1995. In addition, new standards were adopted in 2008 but were not used for this research since the 1995 standards were the foundation for TAD. Yet, a cursory review of the 2008 standards suggests that TAD is in alignment with the revisions. Overall, this evaluation study, in combination with prior reports (Population Health Institute, 2008) sponsors that TAD is operating in an effective manner that could be improved through increased and stable community resources, criminal justice agencies, and funding.

References

Abram, K.M., & Teplin, L.A. (1991). Co-occurring disorders among mentally ill jail detainees: Implications for public policy. *American Psychologist, 46*, 1036-1045.

Clark, J. (2008). A framework for implementing evidence-based practices in pretrial services. In *Topics in Community Corrections, Annual Issue 2008: Applying Evidence-Based Practices in Pretrial Services.* (pp. 3-8). Washington D.C.: National Institute of Corrections, U.S. Department of Justice. Retrieved from http://static.nicic.gov/Library/022904.pdf

Dillman, D. A. (2007). *Mail and internet surveys: The tailored design method (2 ed).* Hobokon, NJ: John Wiley & Sons, Inc.

Green, K., Smith, P, & Bryant, K. (2008). Advancing evidence-based practices in the pretrial field. In *Topics in Community Corrections, Annual Issue 2008: Applying Evidence-Based Practices in Pretrial Services.* (pp. 10-12). Washington D.C.: National Institute of Corrections, U.S. Department of Justice. Retrieved from http://static.nicic.gov/Library/022904.pdf

Hankey, B. M. (2008). Pretrial defendants: Are they getting too much of a good thing? In *Topics in Community Corrections, Annual Issue 2008: Applying Evidence-Based Practices in Pretrial Services.* (pp. 18-20). Washington D.C.: National Institute of Corrections, U.S. Department of Justice. Retrieved from http://static.nicic.gov/Library/022904.pdf

Mauer, M. (2001). The causes and consequences of prison growth in the United States. *Punishment & Society, 3*, 9-20.

National Association for Pretrial Services Agencies. (1995). Performance standards and goals for pretrial release and diversion. Retrieved from http://www.napsa.org

National Institute of Corrections, U.S. Department of Justice. (2008). *Topics in Community Corrections, Annual Issue 2008: Applying Evidence-Based Practices in Pretrial Services.* (2008). Washington D.C.

Newcomer, K. E., Hatry, H. P., & Wholey, J. S. (1994). Meeting the need for practical evaluation approaches: An introduction. In Wholey, J. S., Hatry, H. P., & Newcomer, K. E. (eds). *Handbook of practical program evaluation* (pp. 1-10). San Francisco, CA: Jossey-Bass Publishers.

Ogloff, J. R., Roesch, R., & Hart, S. D. (1994). Mental health services in jails and prisons: legal, clinical, and policy issues. *Law and Psychology Review, 18,* 109.

Population Health Institute, University of Wisconsin. (2008). *Treatment alternatives and diversion (TAD) program: Report on participant outcomes.* Madison, Wisconsin: VanStelle, K., & Goodrich, J.

Scheirer, M. A. (1994). Designing and using process evaluation. In Wholey, J. S., Hatry, H. P., & Newcomer, K. E. (eds). *Handbook of practical program evaluation* (pp. 40-68). San Francisco, CA: Jossey-Bass Publishers.

Staton-Tindall, M., Havens, J.R., Oser, C.B., Prendergast, M., & Leukefeld, C. (2009). Gender-specific factors associated with community substance abuse treatment utilization among incarcerated substance users. *International Journal of Offender Therapy and Comparative Criminology, 53,* 401-419.

Steadman, H. J. & Naples, M. (2005). Assessing the effectiveness of jail diversion programs for persons with serious mental illness and co-occurring substance use disorders. *Behavioral Sciences & the Law, 23,* 163-170.

Steadman, H. J, Osher, F. C., Robbins, P. C., Case, B., Samuels, S. (2009). Prevalence of serious mental illness among jail inmates. *Psychiartric Services, 60,* 761-765.

The Crime and Justice Institute and the National Institute of Corrections, Community Corrections Division. (2007, April). *Legal and evidence based practices: Application of legal principles, laws, and research to the field of pretrial services.* Washington D. C.: VanNostrand, M.

The GAINS Center. (1997). Intervention strategies for offenders with co-occurring disorders: What Works? Delmar, NY: Peters, R.H., & Hills, H.A.

The U.S. Department of Justice, Office of Justice Programs, Bureau of Justice Statistics. (2006). *Drug use and dependence, state and federal prisons, 2004.* U.S. Department of Justice. (NCJ 213530). Washington D.C. Retrieved from http://bjs.gov/content/pub/pdf/dudsfp04.pdf

Weiss, C. H. (1972). *Evaluation research: Methods of assessing program effectiveness.* Englewood Cliffs, NJ: Prentice-Hall Inc.

Appendix A: Open-Ended Questions

1. Think of a recent client that successfully completed the TAD program. Without using specifics (e.g., name, case number, judge's names) explain the situation including why you think the client was successful, the role of TAD in ensuring success, and the outcome of his/her success.

2. Think of a recent client that did not successfully complete the TAD program. Without using specifics (e.g., name, case number, judge's names) explain the situation including why you think the client was unsuccessful, what TAD could have done better to create a successful outcome, and the outcome of his/her success.

3. An integral component of TAD and pretrial diversion is in its connection to the community. List the main benefits for TAD to be connected to the community?

4. List the clients' the main benefits in TAD having a positive connection to community organizations?

5. How could TAD's relationship with community resources be improved?

6. An integral component of TAD is its connection to criminal justice and courtroom participants (ex., judges, attorneys, and courtroom staff). List the main benefits for TAD to have a positive connection to the court?

7. List the clients' main benefits in TAD having a positive connection with the courtroom participants?

8. How could TAD's relationship with courtroom participants be improved?

THIRD PARTY POLICING: IS IT A VIABLE STRATEGY FOR REDUCING CRIME AND DISORDER IN RENTAL PROPERTIES?

Greg Koehle
Lock Haven University

This paper focuses on the emergence of third party policing as a crime reduction strategy in rental properties. The rationale for engaging a rental property manager in a third party policing role is examined, along with the theoretical framework that supports this role. The perspective of the rental property manager on the third party policing role is also presented. The existing research suggests that rental property managers can have a significant impact on crime and disorder in rentals, and that they are interested in serving in this capacity. Suggestions for improvement of the use of rental property managers in third party policing and future research recommendations are provided.

Introduction

Third party policing is a byproduct of the community and problem oriented policing movement of the 1980s and 1990s (Buerger & Mazerolle, 1998). Specific factors such as quality of life policing, the growing practice of civil remedies for crime prevention and control, and computerized crime analysis have contributed the most to third party policing. The need for a third party comes from the inability of the police to deal with certain problems effectively. Buerger & Mazerolle (1998) define third-party policing as:

> Police efforts to convince or coerce non-offending persons to take actions which are outside the scope of their routine activities, and that are designed to indirectly minimize disorder caused by other persons, or reduce the possibility that crime may occur. Though the ultimate target of police action remains a population of actual and potential offenders, the proximate target of third-party policing is an intermediate class of non-offending persons who are thought to have some power over the offenders' primary environment. The police use coercion to create place-guardianship that was previously absent, in order to decrease crime and disorder opportunities (p. 301).

Third party policing can be applied in a very formal fashion, with laws/ordinances specifically aimed at the third party, or third party policing can be more of an ad hoc undertaking where the police engage business owners,

Greg Koehle, Ph.D., is a former police officer with the State College (PA) Police Department. Dr. Koehle is currently an Assistant Professor in the Department of Criminal Justice at Lock Haven University. Dr. Koehle's research interests include legal impact studies, community and problem oriented policing, and crime prevention.

property managers, or other parties who have some real or perceived control over offenders (Mazerolle & Ransley, 2005). Third party policing can also be initiated by neighborhood groups such as the Office of Neighborhood Associations in Portland, Oregon, that helped enact a municipal drug house ordinance allowing the city to impose civil penalties to the property owner where drug dealing occurred (Davis & Lurigio, 1996). Whether third party policing is an informal or formal endeavor, or initiated by the government or community group, there is one consistent feature; the "legal lever" (Mazerolle & Rainsley, 2005). The "legal lever" provides the government with the legal basis to coerce the third party to change the routine activities of the offenders (Mazerolle & Rainsley, 2005).

The two primary purposes of third party policing are crime prevention and crime control (Mazerolle & Ransley, 2005). Crime prevention can be accomplished through third party policing by focusing the third parties' actions toward underlying criminogenic conditions that foster crime. For example, with the current topic of crime in rentals, the police cannot dictate who rents/lives in their jurisdiction. A rental property manager does have some control over who lives in a rental through a legal screening process that could eliminate potential problem tenants that the police would later have to deal with. Additionally, a rental property manager can dictate acceptable renter behavior and punish or evict a tenant for unacceptable activities. The rental property manager also has greater access to civil remedies, which require a lower burden of proof than criminal cases. The contractual relationship that they can establish with a tenant, along with active rental property management practices, all equate to a high potential for crime prevention and control. The following section discusses the advantages of using civil remedies for crime control, examines several successful third party policing programs involving rental property managers, explores the theoretical framework that supports this role, and also presents research on the rental property manager's perspective of this role.

Civil Remedies for Crime Prevention

While the use of civil remedies for crime prevention and crime control has been growing since the 1980s, this practice is not new. Since 1863, the False Claims Act granted Federal administrative agencies the power to impose punitive sanctions in a range of civil proceedings (Finn & Hylton, 1994). Additionally, several states have century-old civil statutes that are now being used. For example, in 1986, the Westside Crime Prevention Association in New York City filed a lawsuit against the property owner of a local crack house basing the suit on a 125 year-old statute enacted for "bawdy houses" (prostitution houses)

(Mazerolle & Roehl, 1998). This statute specifically defined a nuisance property as

> ...any real property used for illegal trade, business or manufacture and outlined civil actions that a property owner could face if the owner does not in good faith diligently evict the tenant" (Mazerolle & Roehl, p. 3, 1998).

This case resulted in tenant eviction and more frequent use of the "bawdy house" statute by the Manhattan District Attorney's Office (Mazerolle & Roehl, 1998). Civil remedies for crime prevention and control can also be used in a variety of areas for a variety of crimes (Cheh, 1991). Examples include, protection from abuse orders in domestic violence cases, hate crimes, chop shop rings, and possession of weapons by the mentally ill (Finn & Hylton, 1994). Civil remedies have also been utilized internationally in Great Britain and Australia (Morris, 1998; Mazerolle & Ransley, 2005).

The use of civil remedies for crime control, at first glance, seems paradoxical, especially considering the great extent to which crime is a political issue. Another irony is that crime is largely a local issue, however the politicization of crime along with immense media coverage have made it a national issue (Marion & Oliver, 2005). Crime bills named in memory of victims and punitive sentencing that demonstrate a tough-on-crime stance are required in this current political climate. Despite the increase in criminal laws and increasingly punitive stance on crime, there are several reasons for the growth of civil remedies for crime control. The primary advantage is that criminal solutions are simply either ineffective or not applicable for some issues (Mazerolle & Roehl, 1998). For example, quality of life issues normally fall under lower levels of disorder and nuisance and may not be enforceable by criminal law. Even if they are enforceable by law, the penalties are nominal fines.

While controversial, another clear advantage to civil remedies is that they are easier to apply due to either a diminished or complete lack of due process rights normally afforded to a defendant in criminal cases (Cheh, 1991). Along the same lines, civil laws require a lower burden of proof (preponderance of the evidence) than criminal laws (beyond a reasonable doubt) which increases the probability of a verdict in favor of the plaintiff (Cheh, 1991). Further, using a civil remedy such as third party policing saves government resources because the "third party" has taken on part of the police role in monitoring and controlling behavior. Finally, Mazerolle & Ransley's (2005) meta-analysis of over 70 third party policing programs for a wide variety of issues (drugs, violent crime, public disorder, juvenile crime, and property crime) found that civil remedies imposed by a third party are effective where criminal enforcement strategies have been ineffective.

There are several interrelated factors that can be attributed to the growing trend of civil remedies for crime prevention and crime control. The first is the change from reactive to proactive policing practices under the community and problem-oriented policing paradigms (Goldstein, 1990). While difficult to define, community and problem-oriented policing differ significantly from the traditional policing approach. Community and problem oriented policing shifted the focus from arrest rates and response times under the traditional approach, to quality of life issues, born out of broken windows theory and an overall shift toward solving and preventing problems (Roehl, 1998; Weisburd & Eck, 2004). Additionally, the creation of new policing approaches such as third party policing is argued to be representative of the fact that police cannot deal with crime on their own (Ready, Mazerolle, & Revere, 1998).

The notion that the police cannot effectively deal with crime on their own was identified during the dramatic increase in crime rates and civil unrest during the 1960s and subsequent Presidential Commission on Law Enforcement and the Administration of Justice. The report published by the Commission, "The Challenge of Crime in a Free Society" (1967) specifically identified that while the police are tasked with solving these problems, they do not have control over the many factors that contribute to the problems.

Evaluation of Third Party Policing Programs involving a Rental Property Manager

While third party policing is a growing initiative, there is little evaluative evidence on the effectiveness of rental property managers in this role. The following section examines the findings of several programs in which the rental property manager assumed a third party policing role.

In October, 1988 the Oakland Police Department created the Beat Health Unit to focus on drug and disorder problems (Mazerolle, Kadleck, & Roehl, 1998). The Beat Health Team consists of a police officer and a police service technician who opens cases on properties based upon repeat emergency calls, several narcotics arrests, and/or requests from the community. Once the case is opened, the Beat Health Team makes a visit to the location and meets with the property manager, which could be a homeowner, landlord, or business owner. At the meeting, the Beat Health Team provides crime prevention suggestions and works toward gaining the confidence of the property manager that the police support an intervention to correct the problem. The Beat Health Team also schedules site visits by the Specialized Multi-Agency Response Team (SMART) which is comprised of a group of city inspectors from Housing, Fire, Public

Works, and Pacific Gas & Electric. SMART inspects the property for respective code violations and takes enforcement actions when necessary.

An evaluation of the Beat Health Program studied the impact of property managers on drug dealing and signs of disorder. The study occurred over five months and consisted of 100 street blocks as the units of analysis, where 50 were assigned to Beat Health and the remaining 50 control sites treated with traditional patrol tactics. Over 3/4 of the locations consisted of rental properties with the remaining being businesses and owner occupied housing. The actions of the property managers in the experimental Beat Health sites significantly reduced disorder and drug dealing versus the control sites that were subject to traditional patrol tactics. It is clear that property managers can play a significant role in reducing drug dealing and disorder (Mazerolle, et al., 1998).

A similar program in San Diego also emphasized the role of the rental property manager. In an effort to address drug dealing in rental properties the San Diego Police Department focused on rental property managers (Eck & Wartell, 1998). It was determined that drug dealers actually seek rental properties with weak management practices. In cases where management practices are weak the police and prosecutors do have the option of nuisance abatement, which involves a civil suit against the property manager to end the nuisance. Unfortunately, this is a time-consuming process that can only be applied to a few persistent locations. An alternative to nuisance abatement is for the police to partner with the rental property manager and assist them by training them on how to detect and eliminate drug trafficking.

To determine the effectiveness of this program a randomized experiment was conducted involving 121 rental property units that were subject to some form of drug enforcement activity from June through November, 1993. The 121 rental property units were randomly assigned to one of the three groups. A total of 42 places were assigned to a control group where no further police action was taken during the experiment. The second group, also consisting of 42, received a letter from the San Diego Police Department's Drug Abatement Response Team (DART). The letter informed the property manager of the recent drug activity and offered police assistance in eliminating the drug dealers. The letter also warned the property manager that continued drug dealing could result in a civil suit filed by the City of San Diego and a possibility of a $25,000 fine as well as the rental unit being closed for up to one year. The remaining third (37 places) received the most police action. The rental property manager received a letter from DART emphasizing the legal action described above that the city could take if the drug problem was not corrected. The letter also indicated that the rental property manager should contact a DART detective or a detective would contact them to schedule an interview at the property. The DART detective and a member from the City's Code Compliance Department then met with the rental property manager to conduct an inspection and develop a plan to deter future drug dealing. After the meeting the detective continued to work with the rental property manager to ensure that changes were made.

To determine the effectiveness of this program, all felony level crime incidents for each site were measured for 30 months following the treatment. At the end of the 30 months, the control group had the highest level of crime, followed by the group that only received the letter. The group that received the meeting and assistance from the detective had the lowest reported crime. This research concluded that rental property managers do play a significant role in preventing illicit activities such as drug dealing.

A slightly different program in State College (Pennsylvania) involved the creation of a Nuisance Rental Property Ordinance specifically aimed at rental property managers (Koehle, 2011). The Ordinance created a point system for crimes committed in rentals. Rental property managers were held accountable for crimes that occurred at their rentals. If a rental accumulated five points in a twelve month period it was designated a "nuisance" and the rental property manager was contacted with the request of developing a corrective action plan that often involved eviction proceedings. If a rental accumulated ten points in a twelve month period the rental property manager lost the right to rent the property for six to twelve months, which resulted in thousands of dollars of lost revenue. An evaluation of the Ordinance five years after it was enacted found that crimes in nuisance rentals were reduced by 55%; again largely due to the actions of rental property managers (Koehle, 2011).

Theoretical Framework for Rental Property Managers

As discussed previously, the rationale for focusing on rental property managers is that they have a contractual relationship with a tenant and subsequently have some power over certain types of tenant behavior (Campbell & DeLong, 2000). While some element of deterrence theory does underlie third party policing approaches, the propositions that property managers have control over tenants as potential offenders, and have control over the rental unit as the place of the crime is likely more fully understood if the recent revisions to routine activity theory are incorporated. Originally, routine activity theory simply proposed that crime occurred when a motivated offender came into contact with a suitable target, in the absence of capable guardianship (Cohen & Felson, 1979). Felson (1986) added the role of "intimate handler," defined as "someone with sufficient knowledge of the potential offender to grasp the 'handle' and exert control" (p. 120). This revision borrows from Hirschi's (1969) control theory; specifically the four elements of informal social control (commitments, attachments, involvements, and beliefs). Felson (1986) argues that these four elements can be summarized into one word, "handle" (p.121). Felson further specifies that in order for the intimate handler to control the offender, they must be close enough to grasp the handle, or elements of informal social control. Felson proposes that people are deterred from violating rules if it would impair future plans, cause family and/or friends to be disappointed in them, and/or the offender's beliefs cause remorse for violating rules. Felson further explains,

> Lacking commitment to the future, attachment to others, or conventional involvements and beliefs in the rules, an individual has no handle to be grasped, and informal social control is impossible. (p.121).

Felson's revision also differs from control theory where it is proposed that a person would not offend based on a personal acknowledgement of bonds, not because of being "handled" by someone else so that offending is deterred or stopped. In the case of third party policing, the rental property manager can handle a potential offender through strict provisions in a lease that outline unacceptable behavior and subsequent consequences. Also, regular inspections of the property and regular contact with the tenants allow for the rental property manager to remain close enough to "grasp the handle."

To Felson's modification, Eck (1994) added the role of "place manager" to routine activity theory. Eck (1994) proposed that

> ...crime occurs when there is a convergence in time of a desirable target without an effective guardian, a motivated offender without an effective handler, at a facilitating place without an attentive manager. (p. 29).

These revisions to routine activity theory show how a rental property manager can be expected to assume a third party policing role.

Rental Property Manager Perspective

The rental property manager is expected to fulfill a central role in third party policing programs that focus on crime in rentals. As mentioned earlier, little evaluative research has been completed on third party policing programs involving rental property managers, let alone gathered the perspective of the rental property manager. The following studies focus on the rental property manager and provide valuable insight to their role and attitude about the third party policing programs.

A 1992 study of rental property managers across five cities (Alexandria, VA, Houston, TX, Milwaukee, MN, San Francisco, CA, and Toledo, OH) that have some variation of a nuisance property ordinance was conducted to determine their attitudes and responses to essentially being the target of these programs (Smith & Davis, 1998). The sample for this study consisted of four or five rental property managers from each of the five sites listed above for a total of 22. The study was conducted by telephone interviews. The study found that the rental property managers were in favor of removing drug dealers from their properties. In fact, half were the ones who reported the drug dealing to the police in the first place (Smith & Davis, 1998). The rental property managers also reported that they were concerned about the abatement notices they received because they were worded in a way in which it sounded as if they were responsible and/or profiting from the drug dealers in their apartments. The rental property managers also expressed a concern for retaliatory actions from evicted tenants. Out of the sample of 22, one case involving a physical assault on a rental property manager was reported. Finally, the rental property managers expressed a concern for innocent people, often family members of the drug dealers, having to move out as a result of the eviction notices.

A larger study of Cook County Rental Property Managers in 1993 showed some differences from the first study (Smith & Davis, 1998). First, the rental property managers reported that tenants receiving eviction notices were more likely to resist the eviction than in the previous study. Half of the tenants refused to move out after receiving an eviction notice, and over a third (36%) appealed the eviction in court. With regard to retaliatory actions by evicted tenants, 18% of the tenants threatened the rental property manager and 8% damaged their property.

A larger study of rental property managers in State College (PA) examined their attitude regarding the third party policing role (Koehle, 2011). A survey was mailed to all 769 rental property managers in State College who collectively manage approximately 10,000 rental units. The survey had a 34% response rate after two mailings. Two of the questions on the survey specifically inquired about the rental property manager's perception of their third party policing role. The majority of the rental property managers reported that they do have the ability to control crime in their rentals, and the majority also agreed that they do have a responsibility as a rental property manager to take actions against tenants to deter or prevent crime (Koehle, 2011).

In all three of these studies, the rental property managers reported that they changed their rental management practices as a result of pressure from the government, and believed that their actions reduced crime at their rental properties. In general, the rental property managers also expressed an interest in assuming the third party policing role. These studies suggest that rental property managers have the ability to prevent and control crime. However, the studies also revealed that effective rental property management practices could cause a financial strain and may also result in additional problems and concerns with regard to personal and property safety.

Discussion and Conclusion

It is clear that rental property managers do have the ability to impact crime in their rental properties. It is also clear from the research presented that they do have an interest in taking on this role. What is less clear is how this process of engaging the rental property managers into a third party policing role is accomplished, along with important issues like proper training and an assumption that their ability to control crime is unlimited. The following section provides insight on these issues.

The first step in engaging rental property managers is to make them aware of the level of crime and disorder in their respective rental properties. Once they have a clear understanding of the level of crime and the negative impact it is having, they should be informed of steps that they can take to reduce and control crime in their rental. One of the first steps they can take is to screen out potential problem tenants. Instituting an application process that involves a criminal history check, credit check, and references is a good starting point. If potential tenants have passed the application screening they should be required to sign a lease that contains specific language regarding specific sanctions such as fines or eviction for crimes committed by tenants or their guests. A rental property manager can also deter and control crime by frequent checks of the property and full inspections of the property every couple of months. These simple, proactive steps can reduce crime and disorder in rental properties (Koehle, 2011).

In addition, it is important to recognize that there are limits to a rental property manager's ability to control crime. Despite the fact that the use of private parties in a variety of regulatory and enforcement roles is a growing trend, little is known about the actual actions they take to fulfill this role. Even less is known about the limits of their actions and any potential abuses they may commit in taking actions in the third party policing role. The rental property manager's actions and the limits of those actions are important considerations for how their role as a third party regulator is defined, the sanctions for not complying with that role, and the ultimate success of the third party policing initiative. Many of the third party policing initiatives contain the "legal lever" which the police or other government agencies can use to encourage or coerce the third party into an enforcement or regulatory role. However, they do not contain any provisions on what happens when the third party exercises their "perceived control" and crime still occurs, thus making the expectations placed on the third party unreasonable (Mazerolle & Ransley, 2005).

Under the third party policing paradigm, the focus is on the enforcement or regulatory function of the third party, such as a rental property manager. However, it should be noted and considered that the rental property managers only represent the proximate target, not the ultimate target, which is the tenant and rental property (Mazerolle & Ransley, 2005). Due to the fact that the rental property manager is not the actual target (i.e., where the actual change or compliance is desired), there is only so much that can be done to control the tenant and what occurs at the rental property. Quite simply, just like other individuals who have a role in preventing and controlling crime, there are limittions to their ability.

The fact that third party policing policy does not address the limitations suggests that there are none, and this could have unintended consequences such as potential abuses from a person in a third party policing role. Not only is this generally unreasonable, it is completely inconsistent with how the positions within the criminal justice system are evaluated. For example, probation officers are not solely judged on the recidivism rates of their clients, they are evaluated on other factors such as the level of service they provide, etc., because they do not have complete control over their probationers. There is a need to define the limits of the rental property manager's role and ability. These defined limits will then determine how their actions will be evaluated.

As discussed above, the rental property manager can take the actions discussed previously (application process, lease, regular checks, and inspections). Outside of these actions, the rental property manager should not be expected to have any other impact. It is unreasonable to assume that the rental property manager would be present in the rental at all times to monitor what occurs. Even if they were present at different times either in a covert or overt manner, they can only be expected to report misconduct to the police, not take physical action to stop a violation in progress. The rental property managers should be judged on how they exercise control over tenants, not whether crime is ultimately prevented and controlled.

Additionally, the scope of their control should be defined by the government or agency calling on them as a third party because of their 'perceived control.' This perceived control should be defined by specific actions that the rental property manager can take, and show proof of taking in the event that crime occurs and/or continues to occur. Again, this rationale falls directly in line with how positions/actions within the criminal justice system are evaluated. The actions of those within the criminal justice system are evaluated based on the totality of the circumstances and what is reasonable, not just on the end result.

For example, if a police officer shoots a suspect for pointing what appeared to be a firearm at the officer in a dimly lit hallway in a high crime area, the officer will not be held accountable if the actions taken were reasonable. The fact that the suspect was holding a cell phone in a dimly lit hallway in a high crime area would likely outweigh the end result because it is reasonable based on the totality of the circumstances. In contrast, it is unreasonable to assume that rental property managers have unlimited crime prevention and control ability and the limitations of their ability, or any third party's ability, should be assessed and understood before asking or mandating enforcement or regulatory action from them. In summation, it is unreasonable to punish or penalize rental property managers for actions over which they have limited or no control.

Future research should explore the limitations of the rental property manager's crime prevention and control ability. Focus should also be placed on the conflict that can occur as a result of effective rental property management practices and the potential for any abuse of the third party policing role. Finally, future research should examine the use of incentives, rather than solely using punishment, as a means to effectively engage the rental property manager into a third party policing role.

References

Buerger, M. E., & Mazerolle, L. G. (1998). Third party policing: a theoretical analysis of an emerging trend. Justice Quarterly, 15(2), 301-327.

Campbell DeLong Resources. (2000). *Keeping illegal activity out of rental property: A police guide for establishing landlord training programs.* Washington, DC: U.S. Department of Justice, Bureau of Justice Assistance. Retrieved from https://www.ncjrs.gov/pdffiles1/bja/148656.pdf

Cheh, M. M. (1991). Constitutional limits on using civil remedies to achieve criminal law objectives: Understanding and transcending the criminal-civil law distinction. Hastings Law Journal, 42, 1325-1413.

Cohen, L. E., & Felson, M. (1979). Social change and crime rate trends: a routine activity approach. *American Sociological Review, 44*(4), 588-608.

Davis, R. C., & Lurigio, A. J. (1996). Fighting back: Neighborhood antidrug strategies. Thousand Oaks, CA: Sage.

Eck, J. E. (1994). Drug markets and drug places: A case-control study of the spatial structure of illicit drug dealing. (Unpublished doctoral dissertation). University of Maryland, College Park.

Eck, J. E., & Wartell, J. (1998). Improving the management of rental properties with drug problems: A randomized experiment. In L. Mazerolle and J. Roehl (Eds.), Civil Remedies and Crime Prevention (pp. 161-186). Monsey, NY: Criminal Justice Press.

Felson, M. (1986). Linking criminal choices, routine activities, informal control, and criminal outcomes. In D. Cornish and R.V. Clarke (Eds.), *The Reasoning Criminal* (pp. 119-128). New York, NY: Springer-Verlag.

Finn, P., & Hylton, M. O. (1994). Using civil remedies for criminal behavior: Rationale, case studies, and constitutional issues. Washington, DC: U.S. National Institute of Justice.

Felson, M. (1986). Linking criminal choices, routine activities, informal control, and criminal outcomes. In D. Cornish and R.V. Clarke (Eds.), *The Reasoning Criminal* (pp. 119-128). New York, NY: Springer-Verlag.

Goldstein, H. (1990). Problem-oriented policing. New York, NY: McGraw-Hill.

Koehle, G.M. (2011). An interrupted time series analysis of the state college nuisance property ordinance and an assessment of rental property managers as place manager/intimate handler of offender. Doctoral Dissertation. Proquest. 3468577

Marion, N. E., & Oliver, W. M. (2005). The public policy of crime and criminal justice. Upper Saddle River, NJ: Prentice Hall.

Mazerolle, L., Kadleck, C., & Roehl, J. (1998). Controlling drug and disorder problems: The role of place managers. Criminology, 36(2), 371-403.

Mazerolle, L., & Ransley, G. (2005). Third party policing. New York, NY: Cambridge University Press.

Morris, S. (1998). A case for partnership: The local authority landlord and the local police. In L. Mazerolle and J. Roehl (Eds.), Civil Remedies and Crime Prevention (pp. 329-346). Monsey, NY: Criminal Justice Press.

Ready, J., Mazerolle, L., & Revere, E. (1998). Getting evicted from public housing: An analysis of the factors influencing eviction decisions in six public housing sites. In L. Mazerolle and J. Roehl (Eds.), Civil Remedies and Crime Prevention (pp. 307- 328). Monsey, NY: Criminal Justice Press.

Roehl, J. (1998). Civil remedies for controlling crime: The role of community organizations. In L. Mazerolle and J. Roehl (Eds.), Civil Remedies and Crime Prevention (pp. 241-260). Monsey, NY: Criminal Justice Press.

Smith, B. E., & Davis, R. C. (1998). What do landlords think about drug abatement laws? In L. Mazerolle and J. Roehl (Eds.), Civil Remedies and Crime Prevention (pp. 291-306). Monsey, NY: Criminal Justice Press.

Weisburd, D., & Eck, J. E. (2004). What can police do to reduce crime, disorder, and fear? The Annals of the American Academy of Political and Social Science, 593, 42-65.

Book Review: *New Directions in Media and Politics*
Ridout, Travis N. (Ed.) (2013). New York: Routledge

Alison Novak
Drexel University

Travis N. Ridout's *New Directions in Media and Politics* should be required reading for all political communication courses. With finesse and great experience, Ridout's collection of chapters cover the most important topics currently effecting political communication practitioners and researchers, ranging from the institutionalized media system to the ethics of Internet news consumption. Ridout's authors provide a wealth of resources, original research, and reflection on important scholarly advancements. In designing the volume, Ridout allowed researchers to make their own thematic chapters surrounding what they feel are the most important issues facing political communication. In doing so, his book truly reflects a multitude of perspectives and new directions.

Several predominant themes appear through the edited volume. First, Ridout begins the introduction of the book by reflecting on the decline of American newspapers and their replacement with online news blogs and editorials. Second, rather than news being produced by an elitist press, it is the everyday citizen who contributes to the creation of news, using social media such as Twitter and Facebook to contribute to mainstream news and spread information. Lastly, Ridout suggests the changes in American media production and consumption will result in profound changes to "political behaviors of individuals and the functioning of governments and democracy" (p. 2).

Amongst the many important findings of the volume are the reflections provided by authors studying the fragmentation of the American public and the news sources used by the public for gathering political information. Drawing from theoretical framework such as cognitive dissonance, selective exposure, and media distrust, it is the process of fragmentation, or the breaking down of the American public into small parts, that has resulted in the public demanding news coverage that fits with their pre-conceived ideas. Ladd writes,

> "Because those who distrust the media are less influenced by new media messages, they instead fall back on their prior beliefs and partisan predispositions to form their current beliefs about the state of the world" (p. 35).

This sentiment is echoed in the articles of Fowler, and Yrupnikov and Easter.

Alison N. Novak is a third year Ph.D. Candidate at Drexel University in the Department of Culture and Communication. Her dissertation research examines representations of the millennial generation's political engagement in the news. Additionally, she has studied the online communication practices of American protest groups such as the Tea Party Patriots, The Coffee Party, and Occupy Wall Street.

Also given considerable coverage throughout the book are the forms and types of new mediated candidate campaigning, both during and outside of the election cycle. Edgerly et al. reflect that social media has introduced new demands of constituent engagement during electoral campaign cycles and the personalization of politics. Using data collected from social media sources, political strategists can target specific segments of the population they want to share a carefully crafted message with. These messages are designed for a number of possible effects such as voting, political information dissemination, and participation. Targeted message campaigns are fully explored in Franz's chapter, who suggests that such microtargeting "has the potential to reinforce voter polarization," reinforcing the warnings given by Ladd's work (p. 126).

Along with the use of social media platforms, negative campaigning has been a massive trend in contemporary politics. Krupnikov and Easter's work examines the "elusive effects" of negative campaigning, suggesting that although the technique is popular with everyone from national to local politicians, very little is known or certain about the effects. Research has indicated that negative ads are, for the most part, contextual, meaning their effects are often mediated by an individual's traits, political orientation, and expectations.

Finally, the volume concludes with Hart's reflection on the prospect of digital politics. Hart suggests journalism's new forms have produced a 24/7 news environment accessible by nearly all Americans. This has made political information both easier and more challenging to get. "The Digital Age makes us feel in charge even when we are not in charge, something that television does as well" (p. 216). This illusion of control and access has influenced political news media's production and consumption in the past ten years, and will likely continue.

Missing from the book are several important topics valuable and worth considering when investigating the relationship between media and politics in the 21st century. For example, the book lacks a reflection on the convergence of entertainment and political news television shows. Jeffrey P. Jones' 2010 *Entertaining Politics* reflects that the satiric genre is now popular with almost every generational group and is becoming more and more the singular source citizens turn to for their political news. With the advent and popularity of shows such as *The Daily Show with Jon Stewart* and *Real Time with Bill Maher,* it seems odd that the edited volume fails to reflect on what this means for political communication and the collective action required for democracy. Also missing is a consideration of political activist groups and their use and representation in the media. Groups such as Occupy Wall Street and The Tea Party Patriots have revolutionized the use of digital news media, but again, were left out of the volume. The book primarily focuses on electoral politics, rather than political activist or protest groups.

Despite these oversights, the book remains foundational for students and practitioners. While the chapters of the book are a good resource for anyone studying political communication, equally as important are the sources used in each of the chapters. Each topic addressed comes with a full bibliography of both classic and contemporary scholarship. This level of documentation and sources is perhaps only matched by Lynda Lee Kaid's (2004) *Handbook of Political Communication Research,* and thus makes it a valuable source for an introductory graduate course.

Visible in the book's design is the care and concern regarding the future of American politics and democracy, exhibited by both the authors and the editor. The text provides readers with an orientation and introduction to a large variety of ontological approaches useful to gain a footing in the political communication field. As a result, the book's chapters do a thorough job describing various positions on possible effects, rather than resting on a singular perspective. This is fully realized in the concluding chapter which states

> "for politics is an ancient thing focusing on ancient needs-land and ethnic sovereignty, scare resources and group solidarity. Politics fights new battles each day but, as the Middle East continually reminds us, it fights old battles again and again" (p. 210).

This book is less about giving a clear vision of the future of politics, and instead about setting up the reader to make their own predictions. The authors implore the reader to use the foundations given to devise their own place and perspective on political communication research, thus placing the future in the reader's hands.